INSIDIOUS

Copyright © 2009 by Memento, Inc.
All rights reserved.

Published by Memento Press
55 Network Drive
Burlington, MA 01803
www.mementosecurity.com

ISBN 978-0-9825272-0-7

Designed by Alphabetica Design
Printed in the United States
First Edition

INSIDIOUS

How Trusted Employees Steal Millions and Why It's So Hard for Banks to Stop Them

By Shirley Inscoe and BC Krishna

We dedicate this book to the committed fraud analysts, fraud investigators, and banking executives who take the challenge of employee fraud seriously—and who are working hard to address it.

CONTENTS

"WE CAN'T BELIEVE IT!"

When good employees go bad—when they steal from the financial institutions that employ them and the customers who trust them—the initial reaction from colleagues and managers is rarely outrage. It's disbelief.

How could the same people who sat around the break room table for years, who met for drinks after work, who became confidantes and friends, who went to weddings and graduations, *steal*? It's a betrayal of friendship, of professionalism, and of the special trust that financial services organizations have to maintain with their customers. It seems unthinkable.

But it's not. As the often-cited wisdom goes, *banks are far more likely to be defrauded by their own employees than robbed by a thief.* Employee fraud is a growing type of fraud, one that triggers billions[1] of dollars in worldwide losses, damages reputations, and can even destroy organizations. It affects institutions of all sizes, from the smallest local credit unions to the largest multi-national banks. Internal fraud has earned its way on to the top ten lists of fraud threats from industry experts.[2] And it's on the rise, fueled by an uncertain economy, turmoil in the banking system, and growing public skepticism and concern. While our main focus is the financial services industry, employee fraud remains a critical challenge for brokerages, insurance agencies, retail organizations, pharmaceutical companies, and other susceptible organizations. So the themes we'll be exploring in these pages have relevance far beyond banking.

---

[1] We explore the complex challenge of estimating employee fraud losses in Chapter 4.

[2] "10 Faces of Fraud: The Greatest Risks to Banks in 2009," *Bank Information Security*, December 9, 2008.

Fraud is in the air

From Jérôme Kerviel, the junior futures trader at Société Générale who fraudulently lost the bank €4.9 billion ($7.2 billion) to Bernard Madoff's notorious, mother-of-all-frauds $50 billion Ponzi scheme, the media is filled with stories of individuals who are misusing their positions to commit fraud and steal money. And still, the first reaction from their victims is disbelief. No one could believe that "Uncle Bernie" would lie to them and steal from them.

Believe it. As professionals deeply immersed in the challenges of fraud detection, fraud no longer surprises us. We think about it much more like the proverbial *black swan*—just because it's relatively rare doesn't mean it's not important, or a critical problem.[3]

What surprises us is that more banks aren't doing more about it. It surprises us that fraud fighters often have to struggle to convince their bosses of the very existence of employee fraud. It surprises us that employee fraud continues to go unaddressed or under-addressed at so many institutions. We're outraged at the lack of outrage. And we're particularly disturbed when rational banking professionals consider employee fraud as just another *cost of doing business*.

Hardly. Employee fraud is a problem that can and should be addressed. Visionary organizations are already reporting impressive results by bringing new solutions and best practices to bear on the challenges of employee fraud. We applaud their efforts, and highlight some of their insights in these pages.

Fraud has a familiar face

We wrote this book to explore the complex challenge of employee fraud and to encourage financial services professionals to find new ways of detecting and stopping it. We want to bring to light the complicated, multi-layered issues raised by employee fraud. After all, fraud is an inherently human problem, one that often

---

[3] Allen Webb, "Taking Improbable Events Seriously: An Interview with the Author of *The Black Swan*," *The McKinsey Quarterly*, December, 2008.

has a very familiar face. Unlike external fraud, employee fraud isn't the domain of anonymous thieves on the Internet. It's the popular senior vice president. It's the trusted branch manager. It's the customer service representative who never missed a day at work and who kept getting promoted. It's the dependable administrative assistant.

It's a fact—fraudsters are often top performers. The same creativity, attention to detail, and intelligence that helps them succeed at their jobs also helps them succeed at fraud. In this book, we look at what motivates them, as well as what you can do to stop them. We highlight a wide range of employee fraud stories, because behind the high-profile stories of Madoff, Kerviel, and other Fraud All-Stars, there are equally disturbing, but more lifesize stories of fraud and its consequences. And more and more stories keep coming to light every day.[4]

Fraud is easy. Stopping it, less so.

Consider the story of Donna Lee Munson, a mother of three in suburban Georgia, and a former assistant vice president at a top regional bank.[5] Living way beyond a salary she called ridiculous,[6] Munson needed money to pay bills, stay ahead of a bad mortgage, and ward off bankruptcy. And like many people who commit fraud, she found that money at work. Munson defrauded her bank by moving funds from certificates of deposit into her own account—stealing $195,000 before getting caught. "It was easy the first time, and then it just got out of hand," she says.

Munson's chosen type of fraud, *self-dealing*, is one of the more popular in the world of employee fraud. But there are plenty of others, from identity theft to general ledger misuse, to fictitious loans. And new employee fraud schemes are hatched every day—fraud is a growth industry, fertile with innovation. And as Munson put it, *fraud is easy*. Take opportunity, add a motivated employee, and you get fraud. Let fraud go on for long—the average is two years from the time

---

[4] We track new fraud stories and fraud trends on our blog at www.bankfraudforum.com.

[5] We've changed small details of Munson's story to protect her identity. We'll hear from her again in an exclusive interview in the Afterword.

[6] After a decade of exceptional performance at her bank, she earned a salary of approximately $40,000 a year.

a fraud starts until it's detected[7]—and the losses multiply. Despite her obvious, unsophisticated fraud scheme, Munson managed to keep her fraud activities hidden from August, 2004 until November, 2007. How? She showed up for work every day, skipped vacations, and intercepted customers who might be her undoing.

In the end, her $195,000 fraud may not qualify as Madoff-esque, but it's still significant. Multiply it by hundreds of fraudsters like Munson, and the cumulative losses add up quickly.

Munson pleaded guilty and faced 30 years in prison. As we write this, she's beginning to serve an 18-month sentence at a federal facility. But a hidden army of fraudsters is still at work at financial institutions throughout the world, taking more money every day, taking advantage of weak internal controls and the trust of their colleagues, manipulating processes and systems to their own purposes—and putting banks and their customers at incredible risk.

A different vision of employee fraud

This is not a textbook, nor is it a conventional exploration of employee fraud. As you'll soon find out, our approach is unusual and our words are often strong and provocative.[8] We feel strongly about the need to address this critical issue, and want to convey some of our passion—and that of our colleagues—in these pages.

This book is for the banks and credit unions that aren't willing to sit by while employees steal. May it help you in your fight to address the complicated and often difficult challenges of employee fraud. And we salute the silent majority of honest employees who resist giving into temptation and take personal responsibility for their actions—every day. May this book strengthen your resolve to protect your company and to respect your customers.

---

[7] S. L. Mintz, "The Gauge of Innocence," *CFO*, April, 2009.

[8] Especially down here in the footnotes.

Fraud Fact: A Definition

Occupational fraud—often called *employee fraud, internal fraud, employee defalcation, or employee embezzling*—is defined as "the use of one's occupation for personal enrichment through the deliberate misuse or misapplication of the employing organization's resources or assets."[9]

We think of it as employees who take advantage of access, organizational weaknesses, and trust to steal from the banks or credit unions that employ them.

[9] "Report to the Nation on Occupational Fraud and Abuse," *Association of Certified Fraud Examiners (ACFE)*, 2008.

EXPLORING THE PROBLEM

CHAPTER ONE

OPPORTUNITY KNOCKS

"Small opportunities are often the beginning of great enterprises."

—Demosthenes

Opportunity is at the origin of all fraud— at retail banks and beyond.

Without opportunity, no fraud can happen. No theft, no losses, no problems. And opportunity isn't limited to those in positions of power. We just tend to hear about their fraudulent behavior more often, when they exploit their uniquely powerful positions and wind up in the headlines. At credit unions, banks, and other financial institutions, there are plenty of fraud opportunities to go around—from teller to vice president and beyond. You may not hear as much about them, but the damage is all too visible to the institutions they defraud.

To begin, let's steal.
Leave the financial services world for a bit and assume that you work in another commercial venture, say a mid-sized software company much like the one where we work. Take a trip through the office, thinking like a fraudster. There's Michelle's purse—she's left it under the front desk while she's at lunch. Grab that VISA card, won't you? Careful no one sees you. Here's another office. Go through the desk. Good news! Mike leaves his checkbook in the top drawer. Rip a couple out of the middle, so he won't notice they're gone.

On to the company kitchen. See that jar next to the coffee machine where people leave donations to buy more coffee? Clean out a handful of quarters and dimes. It's really out-and-out stealing instead of fraud, but why not?

Then duck into your office for a moment and go online. Think fraud. What could you do to *use your occupation for personal enrichment through the deliberate misuse or misapplication of resources or assets.* There's always the old standby, falsifying your expense accounts. You add a couple of lunches at the Ninety Nine Restaurant that weren't really about business, and hope that Gail, your accountant, doesn't notice.

And don't forget about data, since fraud isn't just about money—data and intellectual property that can be sold is also fair game. So open up the company database, the one that has the names and contact info for all your company's prospects and customers. Unfortunately, it's mostly phone numbers and email addresses, not personal information or financial data. But go ahead and copy that data on a flash drive and pop it in your pocket.

Let's take a break and total up your fraud earnings to date:

Item	Possible Value
One Credit Card	Maybe $10,000, if you use it for online or telephone purchases—fraud is just a phone call away. But you better be quick, because Michelle is probably already reporting it missing.
Two Checks	You might be able to drain about $5,000 from Mike's account by forging his signature or generating fraudulent ACH debits using his account number.
Company Data	Not easily negotiable—the competition would simply laugh at you, or call the cops.
Fake Expenses	$75, if Gail doesn't catch you.
Coffee Money	$1.75, and you probably feel kind of bad about this one.
Total:	**$15,076.75**

Our semi-serious fraud journey has some real lessons:

Everyone has a few real opportunities to commit fraud, even if they never take advantage of them.

Fraud is risky *(Did Mike see me in his office?)*.

Fraudsters need to know how to turn purloined data/items into cash or goods that can be conventionally fenced.

You have to be motivated to steal, otherwise why bother?

To be a fraudster, you have to split yourself in two—honest friend and employee one minute, stealthy thief stalking the office the next.

This double life takes vigilance, basic acting skills, and some form of powerful motivation, moral corruption, or justification.

Fraud is stressful.

Bottom line? Being a fraudster at most organizations isn't particularly easy or lucrative. If you have a massive budget, appropriate funds to contractors, are the sole bookkeeper, or have lax oversight, you might be able to figure out a way to misuse your position and commit fraud. But it isn't easy. It's risky. And the opportunities for stealing large amounts of money are limited.

Financial transactions open the door to fraud

But if we take our fraud operation to a bank, credit union, or other financial institution, everything changes. The key enabler? Financial transactions. Every transaction processed represents a unique opportunity to steal money—this is as true now as it was when the moneychangers were thrown out of the temple in Biblical times.[10] There is a broad spectrum of companies that perform financial transactions for customers—from insurance agencies to banks to brokerages and beyond. In short, this category includes any company that holds your money,

---

[10] Matthew [21:13] "And He said unto them, It is written, My house shall be called the house of prayer; but ye have made it a den of thieves."

securities, or even your personal data to conduct business and transactions on your behalf. Or as one bank describes it—"Banking products represent complex services which presuppose a special relationship of trust between bank and customer."[11]

This special relationship and fiduciary responsibility also offers increased opportunities for fraud, since these companies have the assets and confidential, personal information of thousands of individuals in their possession. As financial service firms, they bear a unique responsibility to stop fraud and protect their customers. After all, banks and credit unions are doing more than simply selling goods or services. They're serving other people, performing financial transactions on their behalf, and ideally protecting them from fraud.

Taking fraud to the bank

At a retail bank, even entry-level employees, such as customer service representatives (CSRs), have extensive financial data at their fingertips—data that can be misused or sold easily online. There are hundreds of easily located online resources that would gladly buy credit card numbers, account information, or Social Security numbers. And then there are many fraudulent actions that even a relatively low-level employee like a CSR can take. A CSR can transfer money with just a few clicks, access General Ledger accounts, claim incentives fraudulently, and do much more. All without attracting much attention, as we'll see in the following story of a CSR gone bad.

Note that the names have been changed to protect the guilty.

Janet Thomas likes her job as a CSR at Queen City Federal, a bank in suburban southern Ohio. She comes to the branch an hour before it opens, gets her consignment items—money orders, traveler's cheques, gift cards, and other items—from the vault. She chats with her branch manager, Bob Durkee, and her co-workers—they all know each other well. This branch doesn't have the turnover

---

[11] "Eurobarometer Confirms that Europe Has Satisfied Bank Customers," *Talking Points*, Deutsche Bank Research, February 13, 2009.

that downtown banks have. And they all spend a fair amount of time together after work.

Janet is relatively new to banking, but she's been at Queen City for three years now and is doing really well—regular raises and commendations. She's never late. She never misses a day, and everyone likes her. She schedules the other CSRs, takes over when Bob has to go downtown for a meeting, and is on her way to a branch manager job of her own in a few years.

Throughout Janet's day at the bank, she's great with customers, solving problems with their accounts, helping them with check and card orders, taking loan applications, transmitting stock certificates to the brokerage unit, and selling consignment items. She achieves her sales goals, performs well in incentive campaigns, and keeps customers happy.

Over the course of her day, Janet has constant access to General Ledger accounts and other core systems. She can debit or credit customer accounts and/or make maintenance changes to these accounts. With a co-worker, she empties deposits and reloads cash cartridges for the ATM. She processes paperwork like a champ and rarely makes errors.

She works overtime during lunch, catching up on her paperwork while others head out to Frisch's Big Boy. After all, she has more to do than most CSRs at the bank. When a General Ledger ticket, debit memo, or loan amount goes over her authorized limits, she usually looks for Bob to get his approval signature. But the bank is in merger talks with Buckeye Bank, and he's often downtown in meetings. He's told her to just go ahead and apply his initials, since he hates to come back to the office to find a stack of work to go through, evaluate, and sign. Plus, he doesn't like to hold things up. So Janet takes care of all of these details, which Bob really appreciates. His mind is on surviving the merger.

Her day ends with a good-bye to everyone, a reminder to go to a wedding shower next week, and a promise to bring cookies in tomorrow.

She turned to fraud, rationalizing—at first —that she would pay it all back.

Finding fraud among the camaraderie

After the merger is complete, Bob Durkee moves on to a headquarters job downtown. Queen City Federal's operations are moved to Buckeye Bank's core banking platform. Unknown to Janet, Buckeye Bank has an employee fraud monitoring system in place. And her new boss, a less trusting manager from Buckeye Bank, soon hears surprising news from an internal fraud analyst— Janet isn't the perfect employee that she seems to be. In fact, she's a veteran fraudster, committing at least two types of fraud.

Among the paperwork that Janet so nicely handled for Bob were fictitious loans set up for her own benefit. She's also been debiting dormant accounts (usually elders) and transferring the money to her own account. And remember those incentive awards? Janet has been opening accounts and manipulating the product codes to achieve the target and earn extra money. Then she shut the accounts down later, knowing that the incentive awards were not tied to the longevity of the new accounts.

Janet's new manager traces her activities back for at least two years. Total estimated losses for her fraud activities alone total approximately $500,000. Why did she do it? Her husband lost his job two years earlier and her income alone wasn't enough to cover their mortgage. So she turned to fraud, rationalizing— at first—that she would pay it all back as soon as her husband found a job. What tripped her up? Abnormal and suspicious credits to an account she controlled triggered alerts from Buckeye Bank's vigilant fraud-detection system—and action from her new manager.

Her co-workers express disbelief, of course. After all, Janet was their friend as well as a colleague. You can pretty much assume that co-workers are always shocked when fraud comes to light. After all, if they were suspicious, they would have called a hotline. The bank's customers are also worried. If Janet is a thief, then others in the bank can be. After Janet's story winds up in the *Cincinnati Enquirer*, a dozen or so switch banks, management is distracted, and the branch has to explain this embarrassing event over and over.

As stories like Janet's show, anyone can be a fraudster. Particularly when they work in retail banking. And CSRs aren't the only potential fraudsters. The cast also includes branch managers, consumer lenders, back-office personnel, tellers, telebanking personnel, vice presidents, the Human Resources department, and even loss prevention officers—the very people tasked with fighting fraud losses. If an employee has access to any financial data or transactions, then they have the opportunity to be a fraudster, which includes almost everyone in most banks and credit unions.

A partial menu of CSR fraud opportunities

Janet's fraudulent activities cover only a fraction of the fraud that she could have committed. Not long ago, our colleague Paul Whitelam [12] started cataloging the actual employee fraud types we found at banks and credit unions. The list stretches on for pages. Employee fraud is pretty remarkable in its comprehensiveness and creativity—*so many ways to steal!* Here are just a few common among CSRs:

Self-dealing—Employees operating on their own accounts to realize financial benefits. A good example is increasing their overdraft limit or depositing money into their own account.

Misuse of position—Janet certainly did a lot of this by performing fraudulent transactions on dozens of accounts, establishing bogus loans, and more.

General Ledger misuse/abuse—Examples include fee or service charge reversals, debits to income accounts, moving money between suspense or in-process accounts repeatedly to avoid detection, and many more.

---

[12] Paul, our vice president of product management, is British, very smart, thorough, and polite.

Bank employees can be coerced, extorted, or recruited specifically to take part in fraud.

Cash disappearance—This category includes taking cash from the teller drawer, removing money from the vault, mishandling deposits, or cash missing from ATM or night-drop deposits.

Sales manipulation—Also known as *incentive fraud*. Janet performed this by making it look as if she had opened accounts when they were simply ghost accounts that helped her achieve her goal and earn the incentive.

Account takeover—This type of fraud involves gaining control of a customer account via deception, then stealing from it. This form of identity theft is often enabled by an employee selling customer data.

Consignment items fraud—A CSR can steal travelers checks, official bank checks, money orders, gift cards, and more items assigned to them, then use these items for personal gain.

Collusive fraud—Bank employees are often just part of an external team, working with experienced fraudsters targeting the banking system. Bank employees can be coerced, extorted, or recruited specifically to take part in fraud, providing a valuable *inside man* to perpetrate or cover up schemes.

These fraud schemes are just the beginning. There are many more, and new types of fraud emerge every day as employees like Janet leverage their creativity and knowledge of banking systems to take advantage of the trust of their co-workers, lax oversight, and internal control weaknesses. Fraudsters are adept at turning weaknesses into opportunities. There are many opportunities for fraud, some obvious, some incredibly devious—but all generate losses.

What factors help fraud happen?

Why was Janet able to get away with fraud, and for so long? The reasons are clear, and common at many retail banks and credit unions:

She was trusted—No one had any idea about her problems or suspected her of fraud. She was hard-working, dependable, and always willing to lend a hand, so no one was ever suspicious.

The environment was ripe for fraud—People working together as a team are naturally trusting, particularly over long periods of time.

She was smart—She took fairly small amounts over a long period of time, and via fraud schemes that were fairly invisible to the casual observer, though captured in the transactional data. [13]

Management was distracted—Mergers, financial turmoil, and other outside forces can distract normally vigilant managers.

Internal controls were lax—Normal approval processes, managerial responsibilities, and chains of command were ignored and violated.

She covered her tracks—By showing up every day, Janet could keep her eye on any surprise audits or other potential threats to her hidden work. There was no suspicious paperwork in her drawer, no flashy jewelry, no fancy cars. Everything looked normal.

These are just a few of the reasons why fraud flourishes at financial institutions. Many people have access to key systems, and statistically, some of them are going to have the opportunity to steal—and the all-important motivation (which we'll explore in more detail in the next chapter).

---

[13] We'll be exploring the value of data in more detail in Chapter 8.

Technology creates new opportunities

It's important to point out that technology plays a role in providing new opportunities for fraud. Not long ago, retail banking moved more slowly, relied more on paper, had more review processes, sign-offs, and generally more obstacles to fraud than opportunities. In a laudable move to improve customer service, banks opened up access to key customer data to a wider spectrum of bank personnel, including telebanking personnel, off-site or outsourced customer service groups, and more.

It's simple. More access equals more opportunities for fraud. And technology is the enabler, since computer keystrokes are the most common employee fraud tool. But technology enables new fraud opportunities in many other ways:

Electronic entries have replaced many paper documents that required two signatures (e.g., General Ledger entries, debit and credit advices). Paper documents invited more scrutiny or questions prior to approval, perhaps since they required a physical signature.

Online/remote access lets bank personnel commit or cover up internal fraud even when they're not on the job. Think of it as *telecommuting for fraudsters*. It also enables bank personnel to work in collusion with outside fraudsters, a growing trend.

Internet data marts provide a willing and lucrative sales channel for purloined customer account data. "There's a huge black market for customer account data," says Avivah Litan, a Distinguished Analyst at Gartner, Inc. "And bank accounts sell for the most money."[14]

Inexpensive and efficient storage devices let employees walk out of work with key data for thousands of customers on a portable storage drive no bigger than a lighter.

---

[14] "Wachovia on Insider Fraud: Prevention and Prosecution," *American Banker*, January 11, 2008.

A visit to the Bureau of Engraving and Printing

To conclude our exploration of the many opportunities for fraud, let's visit the Federal Bureau of Engraving and Printing for a few minutes. The Bureau prints billions of dollars in banknotes every year. And there are more than 2,100 employees in its Washington, DC and Fort Worth, Texas locations.

Within these enormous facilities, millions of dollars are literally at the fingertips of hundreds of employees. It sounds like the ultimate opportunity for fraud. But in fact, the Bureau has almost zero fraud or theft, according to Claudia Dickens,[15] manager of the Bureau's Division of External Affairs. It's important to note that to even talk to Dickens, first we had to write her a signed note on our company letterhead. There are barriers to access, and to fraud opportunities, at every turn within the Bureau.

Exploring the *two-man rule*

"Our employees undergo extensive background checks by the Office of Personnel Management before coming on board," she says. "They also go through further checks whenever necessary, such as when promoted or reassigned." These careful background checks go beyond normal screening for most banks, which rely on a steady stream of employees to fill entry-level positions. And unlike banks, the Bureau has very low employee turnover.

What about monitoring? "Especially in the areas where currency is located, there are numerous security checks, such as badge readers and strategically located cameras." Then Claudia utters a phrase that puzzles and intrigues us. "This is all in addition to the two-man rule."

---

[15] We're pretty sure that this isn't her real name—again, another barrier to fraud.

So what is this *two-man rule?* "No one person is alone when handling currency or entering or leaving an area where currency is located," Dickens tells us. "Documents involving currency are signed off on by both individuals." And these individuals rotate, so it's rarely the same two people working together.

The two-man rule seems like an incredibly simple fraud-prevention solution— one that would be impossible (both logistically and financially) to implement at banks, where employees perform many transactions solo, and where oversight is often automated. Oversight and transactional approvals may try to introduce the same effect as the two-man rule. In fact, some ATM and vault protocols and other banking processes (e.g., approvals for checks or loans beyond an employee's authorized limits) require dual control. Nothing deters fraud faster than scrutiny, particularly in the form of a co-worker watching over your shoulder. Think of it as a *duplexed conscience.* One participant may have fraud on his or her mind, but probably not both.

Though the Bureau is far from the retail banking sector, its solution for employee fraud is intriguing:

Careful background screening of all new hires

Regular, ongoing screening of all employees

Low turnover (inspired by more-than-competitive salaries and benefits)

Careful access control

Constant, proactive monitoring of all personnel (via cameras and sensors)

Regular and vigilant auditing of key personnel and departments

The *two-man rule*

Careful inspection of all personnel entering or leaving the facility

Clearly, this degree of vigilance wouldn't be cost-effective or possible in retail banks. But some of the themes—particularly proactive monitoring—have resonance with the challenges of employee fraud within retail banking.

We'll revisit this concept more in the second half of the book, when we envision solutions to employee fraud. But first, one final insight from our visit to the Bureau. As Dickens points out at the end of our conversation, "it's important to remember one key difference between the Bureau and retail banks—we only have one customer, the Federal Reserve Bank." If banks had one customer, detecting fraud would be more of a priority, and easier to accomplish. But banks can have thousands or millions of customers. And each of those relationships translates into many transactions, almost all handled electronically, many by one person (no *two-man rule*). The Bureau may move a lot of money, but it's on pallets, not online.

To summarize our continuum of opportunities:

	Transactions	Opportunities	Monitoring	Risk
Banks and Credit Unions	Many	High	Some	High
Most Companies	Few	Low	Some	Low
Bureau of Engraving	Very Few	Very Low	Extensive	Very Low

It's clear that transactions equal opportunities, and opportunities lead to fraud. But not without a critical element—motivation. In our next chapter, we'll examine the important reasons why normal employees might become fraudsters—in short, the motivations that encourage *good employees to turn bad.*

CHAPTER TWO

MOTIVATION SETS FRAUD IN MOTION

"Things gained through unjust fraud
are never secure."

—Sophocles

Many people in financial services organizations have the opportunity to commit fraud.

Each computer is a gateway to myriad opportunities for self-gain. Every transaction employees perform includes opportunities to take advantage of their position and knowledge. And fortunately, the vast majority of employees *just say no* to fraud. They may be completely honest, unwilling to commit fraud, or simply scared of getting caught. But most of all, they lack the all-important *motivation* to commit fraud.[16]

There is a human element to all fraud. There are plenty of people who are motivated to commit fraud, and their motivations are powerful and varied. Their motivation fuels fraud. It's one side of the often-cited Fraud Triangle.[17]

---

[16] "Managing Fraud in a Downturn," Special Report Publishing, *The Daily Telegraph* (UK), May 18, 2009.

[17] Developed by noted criminologist Dr. Donald Cressey. Planes disappear into the Bermuda Triangle. Revenues disappear into the Fraud Triangle.

Opportunity opens the door to fraud. But motivation lures employees through it. Motivation encourages CSRs, branch managers, senior executives, and others to take actions that they know are wrong, but that offer financial rewards. No matter what type of fraud they commit, it starts with a combination of opportunity and motivation.

When we ask Paul McCormack, a veteran fraud investigator, about what motivates people to commit fraud, a long exhale echoes over the phone line. "Well, there are so many," he says. "That's what makes fraud fascinating and complicated. It's all about human nature." According to McCormack, the motivation to commit fraud ranges from simple to complex. "People are often under extraordinary financial and personal pressure. They're in debt. They're having an affair. They're in with the wrong people. They're addicted to something. It really is a remarkable range of human behaviors."

McCormack's long career in fraud-fighting includes stints at Delta Airlines, PricewaterhouseCoopers, and most recently, as Vice President of Fraud Detection and Investigation at SunTrust Bank. He's investigated and interviewed hundreds of fraudsters and heard them confess, brag, break down and cry, and even lose their lunch during an interrogation.

What he hasn't heard is the same story twice. The motivation for fraud is as varied as the employees who commit it. That said, there are some general categories that help us explore the reasons why people commit fraud:

People Under Financial Stress. An employee may be about to go bankrupt, trying to avoid foreclosure, or facing a major expense—from an essential home repair to a child who needs a vital operation. These personal needs may be completely legitimate, significant, and poignant—but they're also a powerful motivation to commit fraud.

Addicts. An employee can be addicted to drugs, alcohol, shopping, gambling, travel, a lavish lifestyle, or any other of the many temptations of the modern world. A branch manager who never wears the same outfit twice, a CSR driving a Jaguar, an administrative assistant who takes her vacations abroad (or at casinos)—these may seem like obvious warning signs. But friendship has a remarkable power to render colleagues blind to potential misuse of position and power.

Organized Crime Connections. A fraudster may not be in it alone. They may have a link, even a romantic relationship, with someone in the business of defrauding banks. The employee could have been targeted and recruited to serve as an *inside man or woman* on an organized crime scheme. Or they could even be forced or extorted into participating in a fraud scheme against their will—a growing problem as collusive fraud gangs become more prevalent. No matter what its origins, more internal-external fraud is happening than most banks would like to admit—or know about.

Employees with Bad Attitudes. Some fraudsters simply hate their manager or their employer and see fraud as a way to get even. These disgruntled employees may feel underappreciated, under-compensated, or overlooked. They may not like a merger or other organizational development. They may just be malicious. All these factors contribute to a feeling that an institution somehow *owes* them something. To the fraudster, fraud becomes less about stealing and more about punishing the organization. But the damage and losses are the same.

Thrillseekers. For some, getting away with fraud is a transformative thrill. The risk of getting caught makes it even more thrilling. They may consider themselves smarter than their colleagues or bosses. For these fraudsters, money is just part of the reward. It's the ability to outsmart people and systems. Maybe they've been watching *Ocean's Eleven* too often. Maybe they never learned to distinguish between right and wrong as children. Maybe they're sociopaths. But again, the end result is losses—for banks and the customers they serve.

Motivation by the numbers

A recent KPMG, LLP Fraud Survey[18] took a careful look at who is most likely to commit fraud. This survey of Canadian fraud cases found that:

75% of fraudsters are men

Most have worked at their employer for 3–5 years

Fraudsters are between the ages 30–49

69% of the fraud was internal, 20% external, and 11% involved both

73% of these fraudsters worked alone, 27% worked in collusive networks

Personal need motivated 28% of these frauds

Bad habits (alcohol, drug abuse, gambling) were a factor in 11% of reported cases.

This survey highlights several interesting points. The gender bias, with more male fraudsters, may vary by country, region, location, or industry, since most experts agree that fraud is equally attractive to men and women. And in U.S. retail banking, the employee population is heavily skewed toward women, so we can probably assume there are plenty of female fraudsters.

As shown by these findings, fraudsters are often well-established employees, not new hires, since it takes a certain amount of time and experience to gain trust, identify weaknesses in the processes and systems, and begin to exploit them. And finally, it's interesting to see that personal need—a broad, encompassing motivation—clearly leads the way to fraud, not necessarily the more headline-grabbing category of addiction.

---

[18] "Profile of a Canadian Fraudster: *Survey Report 2009*," KPMG LLP.

Fraudsters are people too

But it's important to look beyond statistics when exploring the motivations for fraud, since they are often heartbreakingly human. It's very easy to demonize fraudsters and lump them in with common thieves and criminals. But consider the recent story [19] of Anna Parsons, 22, of Crawley, a city south of London. Parsons is a young mother with a 3-year-old son at home. She worked at a Barclays Bank branch office on High Street, where she had access to hundreds of customer accounts while working as a personal banker. She used fake passport numbers and security details to set up two fictitious accounts. She then targeted a dormant account and transferred more than £10,000 into the fake accounts, then into her own account.

"Her difficulties began after she and her husband separated," said her lawyer, Graham Pithouse, during her trial, after her fraud was detected. "She was left with no money and a number of debts. She could not even afford to pay the rent. She was in a state of desperation." Parsons is now out on bail, awaiting sentencing.

Parson's case shows how personal need can quickly become motivation for fraud. Consider her situation—she had bills to pay, a 3-year-old son to care for, and a difficult breakup with her husband. It's hard not to feel empathy for her, despite the fact that she also gave into temptation. At work, she also had fast access to the banking systems that can be used to take care of customers, or misused to commit fraud. The powerful combination of opportunity (her role at the bank) and motivation (her overwhelming personal needs) led her to commit fraud. The sad fact is that there are thousands of Anna Parsons working at banks and other financial institutions—motivated people with easy access to other people's money and information.

---

[19] "Crawley Mum's £10,000 Bank Fraud," *Crawley.co.uk*, April 1, 2009.

Low-level fraudsters can do a lot of damage, since there are so many of them. And the losses aren't necessarily small.

Motivation leads to justification

Her case also shows how easy it is to commit fraud. Dormant accounts are a perennial fraud favorite, the *low-hanging fruit* of the fraud world. Creating fake accounts isn't exactly rocket science either, using stolen, fictional, or synthetic identities. And transferring funds takes a couple of keystrokes at the computer. Then the problems are solved, the debts paid.

Unfortunately, it's not that simple.

Most employee frauds start small, as Parsons did, *a few hundred here, a few hundred there*. But it adds up over time. Low-level fraudsters can do a lot of damage, since there are so many of them. And the losses aren't necessarily small. For example, two Delaware men recently pleaded guilty to serving as inside men in a credit-selling scam that cost Bank of America more than $9 million.[20] A father-son criminal ring paid them $500 to $2,000 per list of customers. The fraudsters increased the credit limits of the "customers" (actually, other fraudsters connected with the crime ring) on the list by $25,000 to $50,000. The customers then maxed out their cash advances and disappeared.

This story has it all—collusive networks, small changes that trigger big losses, and an *inside man* angle. The motivation? Payments. The end result? Both participants face up to 30 years in prison and fines of $1 million.

---

[20] "Man Pleads Guilty to Bank Fraud," *Delaware News Journal*, February 26, 2009.

Taking fraud to the managerial level

Higher-level employees can do even more damage. "Without question, the higher level the fraudster, the larger the dollar losses they're able to cause," says a former bank vice-president. "Higher authority levels, such as official checks and lending limits, mean larger opportunities for fraud. Plus, lower-level employees have more internal controls on them, and these controls are generally applied more vigorously."

Lavish tastes inspire an ongoing fraud

Consider this example. Thomas Fetzer is a branch manager at Union Trust in Carmel, California.[21] Fetzer worked his way up to the role after years as a CSR, then a Teller Supervisor. He spends most of his day in his office at the branch, located in a pricey shopping area. Co-workers who stop in to talk to him—for example, asking for approval of transactions over their individual limits—invariably find him friendly and helpful. He's always available. He never misses a day.

As a manager, Fetzer has access to almost all of Union Trust's systems—including the Customer Information System (CIS), Demand Deposit Accounts (DDA), Savings, Time Deposits, Consumer Loans, Credit Card, Commercial Loans, General Ledger, Wire Transfers, Expense Reporting, and more. In short, he's at the center of the branch's operations, so he needs ready access to all systems. And there aren't many processes or internal controls in place to monitor him.

Occasionally, when he needs to book a loan and disburse the proceeds, or perform another similar transaction, he taps one of the CSRs to prepare the official check. He tends to go to the most junior CSRs—to give them experience, he says.

The bank has regular surprise drawer counts for its tellers, which Fetzer announces and oversees.

---

[21] Again, names changed to protect the guilty.

Branch operations continue smoothly until the slow month of August, when Fetzer takes a week off to travel to San Francisco. Looking for a missing file, a CSR spends a minute at Fetzer's desk and uncovers a stash of official checks, each made out to Big Sur Enterprises, a company she hasn't heard of. On a whim, she checks the phone book and finds no listing. The CSR hesitates—after all, Fetzer is a friend, and her boss—but calls the downtown headquarters of Union Trust and checks on Big Sur Enterprises. A few minutes later, it's clear that the company isn't real—it's simply a shell account created by...a Thomas Fetzer.

Fetzer is investigated and his fraud losses total more than $5 million over three years. He's subsequently fired and charged, and in the course of his investigation, his motivation becomes clear—a hidden lifestyle that includes a penthouse apartment in San Francisco, a boat, and a collection of exotic cars. He was driven by the same motivation that leads many to commit fraud—a variant of personal need. Living in an affluent area, he wanted to live more like the upscale customers who walked into the branch office. His desire for wealth and a lifestyle that he couldn't afford on a branch manager's salary motivated him to take advantage of the many opportunities available to him. But his unique position of power helped him hide his fraud for years. Here's how:

Access—Managers have broad access to all systems, enabling them to hide fraud schemes.

Autonomy—Branch managers and other higher-ups are often granted exceptional power and limited oversight from headquarters.

Power—Employees typically hesitate to second-guess their direct managers for fear of reprisals.

Success—The branch was extremely well-run and successful, enabling Fetzer to avoid the scrutiny usually reserved for underperforming branches.

Trust—Fetzer was a member of a tight-knit team, working hard to meet sales goals, customer survey ratings, and other challenges. His teammates trusted him.

Caution—Fetzer kept his lavish lifestyle out of view, avoiding suspicion.

These factors and others enabled Fetzer to steal more money, for a longer period, while attracting less suspicion. His story is about how power can corrupt, if left unmonitored. And it's not an anomaly. For branch managers and higher-level employees, greater access, more power, and less oversight open up new opportunities for fraud—and new temptations. Inevitably, someone has the motivation to take advantage of these opportunities.

A litany of justifications

No matter what the rank of a fraudster—from CSR to CEO—they often find that fraud is addictive, or just becomes second nature. Fraud creates a strong need to justify and rationalize these actions, the final side of the classic Fraud Triangle.[22] *The manager isn't noticing. No one seems to be getting hurt. The account was dormant anyway.* The list of justifications goes on and on. Here are just a few more:

I'm going to pay the money back. It's just a temporary loan.

I deserve the money.

I've been working here for five years and haven't been promoted.

It's just money that's sitting in accounts anyway.

It's not real money—someone forgot about it for years.

These people are rich. They can afford to take the loss.

Our bank is about to get bought out, who cares?

---

[22] Opportunity and motivation are the other sides.

If employee fraud were a disease, it would be an opportunistic cancer, one that grows slowly and steadily.

Our organization is unfair—why shouldn't I punish it a bit?

If no one notices, it's not really stealing.

People around me are losing their jobs even though they've been loyal, long-term employees who have performed well. I may be next!

Justification and rationalization allow fraudsters to keep stealing for months and years. It lets them look their managers and colleagues in the eye in the morning, even though their actions are hurting their team and their employer—and innocent customers. And it enables fraud to thrive and grow. If employee fraud were a disease, it would be an opportunistic cancer, one that grows slowly and steadily, spreading to areas where it can thrive without detection or diagnosis, with one growth inspiring another and another. And while cancer may be motivated by chemical signals, employees are motivated by a range of desires, some obvious, others not.

"The banking culture is based on putting employees in positions of trust and then proceeding ahead with other business," says McCormack, the veteran fraud manager. "Assuming the good in people, that trust is appropriate in most cases. But for others, it's not."

All roads lead to loss.

Opportunity. Motivation. Rationalization. These three sequential stages lead to a final conclusion—loss. Fraudsters may be driven by a range of motivations, many entirely understandable, but the end result for banks and customers alike is simple—they lose something of value, either funds, important data, or their reputation. Preventing fraud by stopping these losses, early and often, remains the real challenge for banks.

"Unfortunately, banks aren't in business to prevent employee fraud," concludes McCormack. "They're in business to serve customers and generate revenues. If they focus on fraud, they're more likely to target external fraud threats. Employee fraud often remains a hidden problem." As well as a major challenge, McCormack might have added, as we'll see in the next chapter.

CHAPTER THREE

WHY IT'S INSIDIOUS

"Acts of fraud—from a single employee defrauding an employer to the large-scale corporate financial malfeasance that dupes millions of shareholders— are singularly insidious. Fraud strips a company of working capital and it attacks its soul." [23]

Insidious is defined as *proceeding in a gradual, subtle way, but with harmful effect.*[24]

Banks face a wide range of fraud challenges—from traditional check fraud to nefarious hackers attacking from continents away. What makes this specific fraud problem fit the definition of *insidious* so neatly? Insiders make employee fraud insidious. Employee fraudsters aren't online strangers in the Ukraine. They're not faceless check forgers. They're colleagues and friends.

Who is the most insidious?

Fraud fighters tend to divide employees who commit fraud into two general camps—*bad from the beginning* and *good employees gone bad*. Both are insidious, in different ways. *Bad from the beginning* employees enter into employment with the specific goal of defrauding a bank. They may be criminally motivated for their own gain. Or they could be recruited to be part of a collusive scheme that involves organized crime—shortly before or after taking a job with a financial institution. Unfortunately, it is becoming increasingly common for crime rings to plant members in targeted financial institutions, and to coerce employees to join them.

This category of fraudsters is growing, according to Catherine Allen, Chairman and CEO of The Santa Fe Group and founding CEO of the US financial services industry consortium BITS. Allen has spent much of her career exploring critical issues in financial services. She sees employee fraud as a growing problem that's increasingly complicated and inherently insidious. "We're seeing more and more organized crime groups recruiting employees either before or just after they take a job at a financial institution," she says. "During uncertain economic times, it's

[23] "Frank About Fraud," *CA Magazine*, September, 2004.
[24] Concise Oxford American Dictionary, Oxford University Press, 2006.

easier to recruit willing participants, and lure them in with the promise of easy money." For these employees, fraud tends to start early, within the first weeks of employment—and it tends to continue undetected for months.

As an example, consider this story:

> A brazen group of thieves enlisted crooked bank tellers to run a shockingly widespread check-fraud scheme that was brought down only when they forged checks on a New York Police Department account. The Manhattan District Attorney's Office is expected to announce the indictments of 18 people—including four alleged ringleaders—although as many as 40 suspects have already been arrested.[25]

Investigators believe that as many as 20 tellers were involved in this elaborate check-forging scam, many placed specifically within targeted banks. Total losses? As much as $2 million. The message? Bank employees can start crooked or be recruited into criminal activities. These employees are insidious because they enter your employment under false pretenses and quickly begin to cause serious damage.

When good employees go bad

The second category, *employees gone bad*, is more subtle, but equally insidious. These employees succumb to the seductive combination of opportunity and motivation, highlighted in previous chapters, and begin to commit fraud. They may have been employed by their bank or credit union for years or even decades. They may have attained high status and compensation within their organization. They may be disgruntled by organizational uncertainty or motivated by one of many desires or problems—particularly during a period of tumultuous change in the banking industry. And they represent a major and insidious threat, since they're difficult to detect.

---

[25] "Fraud Ring in Check: Bank-Scam Busts," *New York Post*, May 27, 2009.

"These people are the most dangerous," Allen concludes. "They know all the systems. They may be really angry. The original contract of trust with their employer is probably broken. And they have power to wreak some serious damage." The more senior the employee, the more serious the loss. In general, executive fraud generates a median loss of $1 million, almost five times the loss from fraud at the manager level, and 13 times the loss per incident created by entry-level employees.[26]

That said, there is no one clear profile of a fraudster. Managers can't pick them out of a line-up. And they probably can't predict who's going to go bad and start stealing. It's just not that easy. After all, if employee fraud were easy to identify, every bank would have solved it by now.

In fraud we trust

Employees who use their knowledge and position within their organizations for their own financial gain pose an inherently different, more insidious threat than external fraudsters. The complex nature of employee fraud hinges on deeper issues than simply taking advantage of their knowledge and position. Employee fraud takes advantage of *trust*—an innate and positive attribute of human nature. Fraud is a perversion of trust that enables an individual or group to benefit financially, fueled by far less positive attributes, such as *greed* and *desperation*. It's demoralizing for any organization, branch office, departmental team, or even family, to see trust overpowered by greed and to see friendship subverted for selfish gain. Exploring these more underlying forces helps us understand why employee fraud triggers disbelief among colleagues, and makes detection difficult for banks.

"Employment begins with a simple expectation of the people you hire—you trust them," says Allen. "People want to trust their employees and colleagues," she says. "It's just human nature. Unfortunately, some employees take advantage of it."

---

[26] "Report to the Nation on Occupational Fraud and Abuse," *Association of Certified Fraud Examiners (ACFE)*, 2008.

Trust creates opportunities

The longer people work together, the more trust grows—as anyone who has worked on a functional team knows. But this closeness breeds new opportunities for fraud. A branch manager might let standard banking controls slide for a colleague because he's a trusted teller. Co-workers might not ever expect that a senior vice president would commit fraud, because of her high position and 20+ years with the bank. At any level, when banks let down their guard, it opens up new opportunities for fraud. And trusted insiders are in the best position to take advantage of them. After all, most people who commit fraud are not brand-new employees. They may have been with the company for months or years—in fact, a recent study puts the average length of employment for fraudsters at 3–5 years.[27] They have had time to develop working relationships, invest in friendships, and make strong, deep connections with their colleagues and managers.

The result is the kind of team bonding that is normally applauded by managers. But if they are motivated to commit fraud, employees can turn this closeness, trust, and shared experience to their advantage—and long-term fraud schemes that drain millions of dollars in revenues and put banks at financial and reputational risk.

"Employee fraud is every manager's nightmare," says one veteran fraud investigator. "Your best employee could be your worst enemy. And you may never know it, until it's too late."

---

[27] "Profile of a Canadian Fraudster: *Survey Report* 2009," KPMG LLP.

A river of denial

Is the perversion of trust at the root of employee fraud's uniquely complex nature, as Allen says? Others are less benevolent about human nature. "The underlying issue with employee fraud is *denial*," says a notorious contrarian —a former high-flying banker with Credit Suisse who has returned to ground as a manager at a financial services firm in Chicago. We'll call him Deep Vault,[28] since his ruthless honesty could cost him his job. "Fraudsters are taking advantage of denial at all levels—from their co-workers to managers to senior executives," he says.

Then Deep Vault quickly turns our questions back on us. "Let me ask you, do you have any real problems? Like a character flaw, some hidden vice, maybe a bad habit or two?" *No*, we answer, since we are perfect—a fact that is widely acknowledged by our families, friends, and colleagues.

"Well, there you go," Deep Vault says with a quiet sigh. "Denial is part of human nature, too. Just like trust. And it's the root of a lot of fraud problems. People want to ignore complicated problems. They're deeply invested in the status quo. They'd rather not know about problems, or pretend to not know about them, than to take the steps it takes to solve them. Particularly if those steps require time or money."

Is employee fraud really that different from other fraud challenges banks face? Is it more insidious? Deep Vault sends out another knowing sigh. "Look at it this way. If you're facing external fraud threats, you can generally create a strategy to combat it. But employee fraud is harder to deal with—and a lot of people would rather not go there. It's complex, messy, and personal. They have enough to do already."

---

[28] Deep Throat, possibly the most famous unnamed source in history, fueled many of Woodward and Bernstein's Watergate stories for *The Washington Post* in the early 1970s. He was later identified as FBI employee Mark Felt, who died in 2008. Deep Vault provides an informed, brutally honest perspective on fraud that we always find provocative and refreshing, sort of. And we'll be hearing from him again.

He then goes on to make a crass but potentially helpful metaphor. "Employee fraud is like the bad breath of banking," he says. "Everyone has it sometimes. Some people have it really bad. But no one really wants to admit it. If they'd just admit it, then they could just eat a mint or something."

If only it were that simple.

A motherlode of malfeasance

The complexity and diversity of internal fraud schemes provides even more proof of its insidious nature. There isn't just one simple employee fraud scheme; there are hundreds. And these schemes can be very complicated. General Ledger accounts alone give rise to an astounding number of fraud opportunities. And new schemes appear every day, limited only by the cumulative imagination of fraudsters. "Insider fraud is definitely getting far more sophisticated," says Allen. "You have fraudsters who know their way around an organization. They know the systems. They know the fraud-detection mechanisms and processes. And they know how to work around them."

Even low-level employees have multiple channels (and related schemes) available to them:

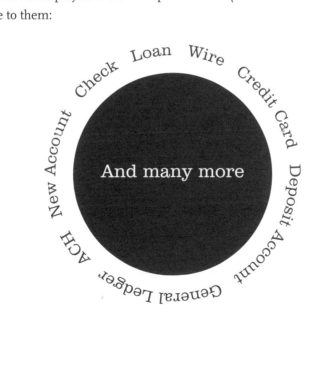

Diverse schemes contribute to an insidious problem

To show the diversity of employee fraud, consider this recent round-up of fraud stories and schemes, pulled from the headlines:

A Wachovia employee in Gainesville, Florida is charged with moving large amounts of currency from the vault to empty teller drawers, then sneaking it out of the bank under her clothing.

Fraudster: Vault manager, working alone

Scheme: Currency theft

Duration: 11 months

Loss: $695,208

A former Bank of America bank manager who deposited $18 million in fraudulent property tax checks is sentenced to jail for his role in a scandal that cost Washington, DC almost $50 million. The District sued Bank of America for $105 million, alleging that the bank failed to properly train and supervise its employees.

Fraudster: Assistant branch manager, working with outsiders

Scheme: Check fraud/money laundering

Duration: 6 years

Loss: $50 million

$105+ million?

Police are searching for a former CIBC (Canada) bank employee who withdrew funds from customer accounts and failed to complete transactions, and also withdrew money without authorization and wired the money abroad.

Fraudster: CSR, working alone

Scheme: Account takeover/wire fraud

Duration: 10 months

Loss: $1.9 million

Employee fraud preys on the vulnerabilities within many financial institutions.

Damage isn't just about dollars

These stories just begin to show the diversity of employee fraud, which makes fighting it a major challenge. The scope of the damage it causes includes monetary losses and reputational damage. After all, rogue, fraud-minded employees can loot customer accounts, book fictitious loans, misdirect funds to others, steal customer data and resell it, aid organized criminals, damage databases, and ruin customer relationships. These insidious actions have a bottom-line cost, but also a reputational impact as well—particularly for high-profile incidents.[29] Lost revenues are just the beginning.

Taking advantage of weaknesses

As one final piece of evidence that employee fraud is insidious, consider how it zeros in on organizational weaknesses and turns them into opportunities for organizational damage. Employee fraud preys on the vulnerabilities within many financial institutions—organizational silos, lapsed internal controls, and other weaknesses. Some experts will tell you that to be successful at detecting and stopping fraud, executives and investigators have to take a holistic view of fraud. They'll tell you that your vision of fraud needs to cross all channels, products, and organizational divisions. Only then can you gain the visibility you need to detect the full scope of fraud schemes and protect your organization.

But this is the kind of advice that makes most bankers yawn, or roll their eyes at its triteness. And it's easier said than done. Many financial organizations remain organizationally siloed, with limited visibility or collaboration across product or delivery channels.

---

[29] We'll be exploring the true cost of employee fraud in the next chapter.

An ever-changing battle against invisible opponents

To provide a way of envisioning what we've learned about the insidious nature of employee fraud, imagine a battlefield where all the combatants are indistinguishable—same uniform, same language.

Banks are fighting an enemy who is cleverly disguised as one of their own.

The battleground is everywhere, stretching from the teller windows to the executive suite.

The enemy has hundreds of schemes and strategies.

The enemy may have help from organized crime.

The enemy already knows the bank's weak points and battle strategy.

The stakes are high—seemingly minor, invisible actions on the battlefield can prove costly or deadly over time.

Sound *insidious?* We think so.

CHAPTER FOUR

THE ESTIMATES

"Fraud, by its very nature, does not lend itself to being scientifically observed or measured in an accurate manner." [30]

Experts tend to agree on a key point about employee fraud—the true cost of this pervasive problem is hard to estimate.

After all, a great deal of employee fraud goes undetected and unmeasured. Some employee fraud is actually characterized as operational losses. And few organizations have an accurate way of quantifying the gray-area losses—such as reputational damage, brand devaluation, and more—that employee fraud triggers.

Employee fraud is often in the shadow of larger, more easily measured external fraud categories, such as credit card fraud or check fraud. However, to diminish the importance of employee fraud fails to take into account the cumulative losses, risk avoidance, and reputational damage.

We often think of fighting fraud as trying to stop heat from draining from a house. You can shut the doors and stop the largest losses. But if you leave the windows open, you're still draining heat/revenues. Ideally, you stop all heat from flowing out of your house, and insulate it from any potential loss. Fraud operates in a similar fashion, except the money you are draining isn't really yours to lose—it belongs to customers and shareholders.

Banks are ultimately responsible for fraud losses. So they should be uniquely motivated to stop all types of fraud, and all levels of losses. That some banks are willing to absorb employee fraud losses as a cost of doing business seems untenable—particularly given the advances being made in fighting fraud. Changing this attitude requires a commitment to fight all types of fraud, one fueled by a clear understanding of the high cost of employee fraud.

---

[30] "Report to the Nation on Occupational Fraud and Abuse," *Association of Certified Fraud Examiners (ACFE)*, 2008.

A measurement challenge

The two most common approaches to estimating fraud are top-down—as embodied by the Association of Certified Fraud Examiners (ACFE) and bottom-up, surveying methods. These approaches are often viewed as two ends of the employee fraud spectrum, with the ACFE overestimating fraud losses and bottom-up estimates potentially underestimating them.

The 2008 Report to the Nation on Occupational Fraud and Abuse, published by the ACFE, found that the typical U.S. business loses 7% of its annual revenues to fraud, creating a total aggregate loss of $994 billion annually. According to this report, the greatest proportion of fraud cases occurs within financial institutions.[31]

However, every organization is different, making application of one across-the-board percentage a problematic approach, one that many feel errs on the high side. And this estimate covers the full spectrum of occupational fraud, from misappropriate schemes to corruption.

Reported losses yield low estimates

For another approach to estimating fraud losses, consider a bottom-up, survey-based methodology, which is used in key industry surveys, such as the Deposit Account Fraud Survey prepared by the American Bankers Association (ABA). This approach is great for highlighting real-world issues and external fraud trends. But when used to estimate employee fraud, it poses some challenges.

---

[31] "Report to the Nation on Occupational Fraud and Abuse," *Association of Certified Fraud Examiners (ACFE)*, 2008.

Banks and credit unions rarely track employee fraud losses in a separate category, making it difficult to extract specific fraud figures that can be attributed to employees. Employee fraud is often intertwined with external fraud, making it difficult to track accurately. For example, if an employee steals data that results in identify theft and fraud by an external ring, are the losses attributed to an employee or external fraudsters?

In short, banks often under-report employee fraud for many reasons—from a cultural unwillingness to recognize the problem to a lack of accurate, comprehensive loss data. And even the most vigilant financial services organizations acknowledge that the insider fraud incidents they detect and solve only represent the proverbial tip of the iceberg. As a result, bottom-up, survey-based methods of estimating employee fraud provide results that are inherently skewed too low.

Estimates vs. reality

If you can't measure a problem accurately, is it still a threat? Yes. Consider this metaphor. Speeding is a problem in the quiet town of Concord, Massachusetts [32] where our company was founded. Is the number of tickets issued by the Concord Police an accurate measurement of the true scale of the problem? Of course not. It simply represents the number of drivers caught by the police. And it's as dependent on the amount of monitoring as the number of speeders. The number of actual speeders is exponentially higher.

So measuring the scale of the employee fraud problem via a survey of reported losses will inherently yield an inaccurate low estimate. And setting a "top down" percentage for employee fraud gives an artificially high estimate.

---

[32] Settled in 1635, much of Concord is still better-suited for horses and pedestrians, not SUVs.

A new way of looking at losses

Is the lack of an agreed-upon scale for the threat of employee fraud a problem? Not really. It just highlights a fact that everyone agrees on—internal fraud is inherently hard to estimate. Let's just admit that the true cost of employee fraud is hard to estimate down to the last dollar, even for experts. What then?

"If flames are shooting out of your bank, do you wait for the expert firemen to come and tell you that your bank is on fire?" says our contrarian, Deep Vault. "No. You jump in and try to put the fire out. Wanting to know the exact cost of employee fraud is just another excuse for inaction."

Ouch. That said, the move to rethink and expand the scope of how employee fraud losses are measured is gaining momentum among more mainstream visionaries. "We need to expand our definition of fraud losses," says Catherine Allen, Chairman and CEO of the Santa Fe Group. "Employee fraud is historically under-reported and underestimated because institutions tend to just look at the dollar losses."

But Allen feels that this more limited way of estimating losses is changing. "Institutions are seeing the impact of events like data breaches, which can reduce revenues by 8 to 10%, and recognizing that other events, such as employee fraud events, also have a direct impact on the bottom line—one that goes far beyond the dollar losses of a specific event."

A real-world approach to estimating the problem

Ultimately, estimating the scale of employee fraud losses at the industry level isn't as important as figuring out how it affects your specific organization. Experts suggest a more broad-based method of measuring the true cost of employee fraud—one that quantifies losses where necessary, and recognizes losses and risks that can't be quantified. Consider three areas that cover the key losses, and that can help create a baseline for estimating the scale of the problem, and quantifying employee fraud losses:

1. Recovering the revenues

> The actual dollar losses attributable to employee fraud (e.g., if $100,000 is stolen, and the margin is 10 percent, then you need another $1 million in deposits to replace the loss)

> Customer migration attributable to employee fraud (e.g., after a specific event)

2. Cleaning up the mess

> The cost of investigating employee fraud and managing risk

> The cost of terminating employees guilty of fraud

> The cost of filing SARs and reporting to *bad employee* databases

> The cost of any lawsuits related to employee fraud events

> The cost of hiring and training new employees

3. Repairing the reputational damage

> The cost of retaining current customers or attracting new ones in the wake of an event

> New advertising/PR necessary to bolster brand and attract new customers

> Repairing other damage to the reputation of the company

"Thanks to high-profile scandals, banks are operating in an environment that is brutally charged."

While the first two categories are generally quantifiable, reputational damage remains the grayest area of losses—and potentially the largest category. "I think the most concerning factor for banks should be the reputational loss to their institution," says Allen. "One employee fraud event can make high-net worth and private banking customers very nervous, or encourage them to leave. And those losses really aren't easy to make up."

Shining a bright light on gray-area losses

Enter Richard S. Levick, Esq., President and CEO of Levick Strategic Communications in Washington, DC, a leader in crisis and litigation communications. Every day, the Levick experts manage the world's highest profile cases—from the latest Wall Street crisis to the Catholic Church scandals. Levick Strategic Communications has managed major fraud and data losses at leading financial firms, giving the firm a uniquely informed perspective on crisis management and damage control. It also makes Levick an extremely articulate spokesman for the true impact of reputational damage.

We called on Levick and Jason Maloni, a vice president with the firm's crisis and litigation practice, to talk about how reputational damage impacts financial services institutions. And we got an earful, as Levick and Maloni issued a wake-up call to our industry. "Bankers really don't realize the level of anger in the marketplace," Levick says. "Thanks to high-profile scandals, banks are operating in an environment that is brutally charged. They need to understand that fraud is no longer perceived as the price of doing business, at least by the public. If you lose $30 million, it isn't your bank's $30 million—it's $30 million from your customers and investors. And you have to be accountable for it. Immediately. Or face the wrath of empowered customers and bloggers, who take their story to YouTube before you've even started to have meetings."

The age of instant accountability

According to Levick, we live in a new age of instant accountability, where consumers hold more of the cards—giving them the power to destroy a reputation or brand in hours or days. Fueled by email, blogs, YouTube, and other democratizing communication and social media channels, consumers can turn one fraud event into permanent damage—the kind that can be measured in many millions. "Let's put it this way," says Levick. "If banks fail to act immediately and decisively, their entire brand can be consumed."

What's changed? "In the past, banking used to be an inherently local business," Levick says. "Everyone knew their banker. As banks become larger, their size and inherent *faceless-ness* works against them. More consumers have little or no emotional bond with their banks. This distance makes it easier for them to turn their anger into action when something disturbing happens—like a major data loss or fraud event." These actions include brand-killing blog posts, boycotts, mass customer exoduses, and more—the kind of stomach-dropping developments that keep bank vice presidents up late at night.

Reputational damage happens faster than ever

Another key factor to consider—speed. "The distance between an event and a critical tipping point is shorter than ever," says Levick. "Crises escalate more quickly now. So banks have to take fast action—in hours, not days." Banks no longer have the luxury of spending weeks or months crafting a response to a fraud event—from a teller stealing customer data to a top executive embezzling millions. They need to act immediately, ideally proactively. Otherwise, they'll be chasing the crisis rather than controlling it.

Looking more closely at employee fraud, Levick and Maloni point to an important factor—there is a villain. "Every crisis is a Shakespearean tragedy," Levick says. "You have to zero in on the villain—the employee who commits fraud—and make it clear that they're being punished." Maloni builds on this theme. "Banks spend millions on various cyber-security measures like the latest firewalls," he

How can mere mortals protect their financial institutions and avoid massive reputational damage?

adds. "But their greatest weakness is their own personnel. Banks need to make it clear that they're investing in protection against employee fraud, acting fast, bringing in the pros, getting rid of the bad guys, and returning to normal," he says.

Strategies for averting reputational damage

Just talking about reputational damage with Levick and Maloni made us anxious. We felt uncomfortable simply highlighting the problem without offering some initial strategies for addressing it. How can mere mortals protect their financial institutions and avoid massive reputational damage? We pass along Levick's response below as value-added advice.[33]

> Know your team now—Identify the lawyers, communications people, crisis management consultants, government regulators, law enforcement contacts, and other key players that you might need to gather together during a crisis. Lay the groundwork for fast communication and collaboration.

> Prepare—Don't wait for a crisis to happen, get your plan together now.

> Network—Know the bloggers and journalists who can make or destroy your reputation, *before* you are in a crisis.

> Take fast action—When an event occurs, respond in minutes rather than days, and decisively, not just with a cosmetic gesture.

> Demonstrate leadership—Make it clear to the public that your bank is taking steps to ensure the highest levels of security. Articulate those steps.

---

[33] Which we hope you never need.

While these strategies don't eliminate reputational loss, they can help mitigate its risk and reduce the length of an event, according to Levick. Does it work? "We're dealing right now with one of the largest data thefts of all time, for a client I can't name," says Levick. "And you'll never hear about it, because the crisis is averted —and the reputational damage will be minimal."

Adding up the costs

So what is the true cost of employee fraud? The estimate varies by institution, obviously. But from what we've heard from experts in the area, the cost is always higher than it seems at first. Once you delve into the details that go beyond dollar losses, you find the cost of employee fraud growing exponentially. On the positive side, clear evidence of this cost can serve as a powerful motivator, encouraging banks to begin to take action—coming up with new strategies for detecting and mitigating employee fraud. It's unfortunate that it often takes a major fraud loss or high-profile, headline-grabbing event to encourage banks to invest in fighting employee fraud, but in the end, they end up stronger for it.

CHAPTER FIVE

VALUE

"Price is what you pay. Value is what you get."

—Warren Buffett

What value do you get out of addressing internal fraud?

At first, this question seems simplistic—you detect and stop rogue employees from taking actions that drain revenues from your institution and its customers. You get the value that equals the sum of the averted losses from those schemes.

But the question of value goes far beyond the bottom line. Addressing internal fraud has an organizational value that is financial, operational, reputational, and even philosophical. In our last chapter, we saw how the negative impact of fraud is significant, even if its costs can't be estimated precisely. Here we explore the flip side—the positive value of addressing the problem head-on.

When we look at value, it's important to recognize that employee fraud is a hidden problem that defies easy solution—so it also defies easy estimation and valuation. As we've seen, it's an insidious, ongoing, evolving, and inherently human problem.

In manufacturing, facilities often post high-profile signs that make proclamations like *540 Days Without An Accident!* that promote safety and advertise how the facility is working hard to address any potential issues. It's unlikely that banks would be willing to post such banners—*101 Days Without a Fraud Event!*

Fraud is too complicated and invisible. A bank can never be really sure how much fraud is happening within the many layers of its organization, the dozens of systems, and multiple locations. There are too many points of entry, too many schemes, and too many variables. And besides, bank personnel aren't machines or machine operators. They're skilled service workers who defy rigid control and direct observation. Variables can't be engineered out of the system. Tolerances for fraud can't be tightened up with the turn of a screwdriver. Banking is an inherently complicated service industry. And internal fraud is about human behavior, a gray area if there ever was one. But that doesn't mean you can't take a focused, Six Sigma approach to solving the problem—one that establishes a fraud-fighting team, identifies and removes the people who are committing fraud, and measures and tracks results.[34] After all, one respected analyst group states that one-third of all internal fraud cases are discovered *by accident*.[35] So a more methodical approach will definitely generate more results—and value.

Building a case for investment

Fraud and risk professionals often find themselves having to build a strong business case for investing in the systems and solutions that can help address internal fraud. We talk to them all the time—well-intentioned fraud fighters who recognize the problem of internal fraud and its impact, but struggle to define it in a way that triggers executive buy-in and financial investment. There is even a detailed white paper dedicated to helping executives build the business case for investing in internal fraud.[36] Clearly, it's important to make sure that funds are well-spent on solutions that generate a measurable return on investment. But developing a business case for focusing on internal fraud can be challenging, since some of the value of addressing internal fraud goes beyond quantifiable projections recorded in spreadsheet cells. But let's start from the bottom line and then move beyond it.

The value of early detection

Addressing internal fraud has both a short-term and long-term financial value to an organization. In the short-term, there are clear financial losses that can be accounted for and averted. A CSR stealing $1,000 from dormant accounts every month allows for simple measurement of the financial impact of her actions, at least during the initial fraud event. But fraud is rarely a one-time event. It's ongoing and escalating. It's a season ticket, not a single game.

---

[34] We'll be talking more about results in Chapter 12.

[35] PricewaterhouseCoopers Economic Crime Survey, 2005.

[36] *Internal Fraud: Building the Business Case for Investment: A Financial Services Industry Briefing Paper*, Santa Fe Vendor Group White Paper, 2007. Downloadable at http://santa-fe-group.com/whitepapers/register.php.

It's a fact. Fraud starts small and grows over time in a fairly predictable loss curve that heads up, not down. As one leading industry consultant puts it: "Whatever the ratio of need and opportunity, embezzlement almost always starts small and grows larger. The need is rarely sated, and the illicit activity usually won't end until the employee leaves the organization, is transferred to a job that doesn't offer sufficient opportunity, or is caught."[37]

Fraudsters grow more aggressive over time, emboldened by lack of detection, escalating financial needs, or greed. So that $1,000 a month stolen by a CSR could have easily trended upward toward $20,000 a month over a fairly short period. So how do you estimate the impact? By losses actually registered before the fraud scheme is detected? Losses avoided further down the line? And what figure do you use—the initial fraud event amount or what it would likely have become without early detection?

In short, there is more value to be gained from addressing internal fraud earlier, even though the actual dollar amounts may be lower. We call it the *value paradox*.[38] By addressing employee fraud more aggressively, the actual losses generated by fraud schemes ultimately go down, making the solution appear to add less value over time.

Data has value, too

Also, consider the value of stopping theft of customer data. An employee printing out data (SSN, addresses, account information) from thousands of customers might not initially register as a loss, under a strict definition. But eventually, this theft can cause significant financial impact, enabling account takeovers that cost hundreds of thousands of dollars, providing a foothold for collusive organized crime schemes, and much more. So there is measurable value in protecting your company from the theft of data, which can be used to fuel many schemes that contribute directly to a loss.

---

[37] Robert W. Jones, "When Bad Things Happen to Good Banks: The Perils of an Unbalanced Internal Control Regime," Santa Fe Group White Paper, 2008.

[38] We explore this paradox in more detail in Chapter 12.

Whether it involves data or dollars, fraud needs to be detected early and pro-actively to reduce its financial impact, and to gain the maximum value from addressing this issue. There is a financial cost to waiting—and a measurable value to catching it early. Few problems solve themselves, and internal fraud is no exception. It metastasizes and metamorphoses. A molehill can become a mountain in very little time. A single rogue employee can catapult your orga-nization onto the front page of the local paper—and not with *good news*. So it's important to factor in the value of early detection when considering value. Bottom line? Early detection limits losses. And ideally, *early* can mean before any losses are generated at all. By strict definition, there would be no *value* in detecting employee fraud when no losses are generated.

Discouraging employee fraud schemes

Now let's look at the less directly quantifiable value created by addressing employee fraud aggressively and early. While fraudsters are creative and elusive, they tend to gravitate toward schemes that work. So behind one event, you're likely to find other similar employees, with similar levels of access, performing schemes that fall within the same general category. Shutting down one fraud scheme—such as CSRs misusing incentive programs—quickly sends a powerful message to other current and would-be fraudsters throughout your organization via gossip, internal emails, and the other invisible communication channels that flourish at banks. *Don't do it.* There are few actions that deter fraud more powerfully than the sight of a co-worker being removed from his or her office by security personnel.

In fact, we just heard from a fraud investigator recently, a former FBI agent, who prefers to schedule these removals for the busiest times of the day, so more co-workers see the end-result of employee fraud—creating a new, in-house ver-sion of the classic *perp walk*.[39] Our fraud investigator isn't promoting this strategy

---

[39] It's important to point out that most firms tend to (and should) handle employee fraud cases extremely carefully to protect the accused and to avoid legal repercussions. We've included this anecdote as an example of how low tolerance of employee misdeeds can send a powerful message throughout your organization.

because he's cruel, but because he recognizes the powerful role of fear in reducing the motivation to commit fraud. He also sees the value of the deterrence factor in exposing employee fraud, early and often. The value of creating the *perception of detection* is that it may ward off other fraud events before they happen, discouraging fraudsters, and ultimately limiting losses.

Efficiency has value

When calculating the value of addressing fraud, it's important to factor in the value of operational efficiency—another hard-to-calculate benefit. An efficient organization, the proverbial *tight ship*, is more profitable—that's Business 101. Traditional financial institutions, such as retail banks, are inherently low-margin businesses. In some ways, that's what motivated many institutions to get involved in riskier, higher-margin businesses, such as mortgage lending or derivatives. But now that the focus is back on performing the traditional, bread-and-butter business of acquiring assets, managing customers, building relationships, and expanding products to meet customer needs—organizations have renewed their emphasis on being as efficient as possible and cutting internal risks and costs, including the cost of fraud. Protecting customer accounts and data (as well as loans, General Ledger accounts, and more) keeps efficiency high while keeping losses low.

Fraud within financial organizations reduces efficiency. It lowers productivity by distracting teams from serving customers and turning their attention to dealing with fraud events. Effective enterprise fraud management boosts overall efficiency and generates value at many levels. It lets operational groups (e.g., branch offices) stay focused on their core business, while fraud detection systems operate in the background to detect and deter internal fraud of all varieties. Effective fraud prevention triggers higher efficiency among the investigative team by empowering investigators to detect more fraud, more efficiently via powerful tools, and enabling fast, efficient forensic investigations. After all, less prevention means more cases, more investigators, and higher costs.

At the executive level, addressing a problem head-on is more efficient and generates more results and value than considering how to address it, or worse yet, reacting to the repercussions *after the fraud has happened and the damage is done*. In short, long executive team meetings wrestling with major fraud events after the fact represent wasted time and money. Damage control has a dollar cost—particularly when you factor in expensive consultants, advertising, and other costs. It's better to stop these events early, or ideally, before they even happen. Ultimately, a more efficient approach to addressing internal fraud early and often brings more value to your organization.

The value of good people, who don't commit fraud

Even the most scrupulous HR processes cannot weed out every potential fraudster. As we've seen, people who commit fraud are people first, fraudsters second. Banks are all about finding good people, and lots of them, to help address the employee churn that characterizes any retail operation. Identifying fraudsters quickly and decisively may trigger some initial costs, such as the cost of hiring and training new people, but your organization gains new value from attracting committed people who are focused on their work and not on their fraud schemes. The faster you can identify the proverbial bad apples, the sooner you can replace them with new, better people—boosting organizational efficiency from the workgroup level to the entire organization. Plus, being known as a company with a low tolerance for fraud helps send a message to would-be fraudsters—*seek employment elsewhere*. Your HR department will thank you for that message.

The value of a reputation

As we saw in the last chapter, financial institutions that experience high-profile fraud events put their hard-earned reputations at risk. It's clear that reputational damage can happen faster and more furiously than ever, thanks to technology and a culture that's quick to destroy icons. But consider the value of your institution's reputation. Where does that value come from? You want current customers to feel as if they're in good hands—that they've chosen the right financial institution to serve their needs. A solid reputation of protecting customers from fraud—by employees and outsiders—helps retain current customers. You want prospective customers to choose your institution over the competition. Addressing employee fraud can play a key role in encouraging customer acquisition and ensuring that in turbulent financial times, your institution remains a *go-to* institution, rather than a *flee-from* organization.

Taking the high road

Examining the value of addressing internal fraud begs a related question—what possible value would there be in *not addressing* it? Not addressing internal fraud problems aggressively is often the easiest route, since it requires no real investment. Institutions can simply continue to check the proverbial boxes that keep regulators happy and hope that nothing major happens that puts their bank in the headlines. It's common knowledge that some executives consider employee fraud too complicated to address cost-effectively—there are simply too many ways for employees to steal. So why bother? Just address the symptoms rather than the disease. Make defrauded customers whole, rather than take a holistic view of employee fraud—one that acknowledges the possibility of a workable solution. Accept the worst side of human behavior and hope for the best. Or just hope (not out loud, of course) that the big fraud losses happen to a competitor.

But this cynical approach to business seems remarkably risky and focused on the short-term. It also raises some serious issues around the special fiduciary responsibility that financial institutions have to their customers—to protect accounts and funds from all threats, known and unknown. If you know that your institution and its customers are at risk of loss—any loss—shouldn't you be *doing the right thing* to protect it? While there isn't an easily attributable dollar value to accountability—to taking the high road and doing what's right— it's a long-term strategy that seems to work for organizations that choose it. And in our era of closer scrutiny of management, executive actions, corporate governance and beyond, accountability has become more than an admirable option. It's become what's expected of organizations that want to attract and retain the respect of their customers—as well as their deposits and ongoing business.

CHAPTER SIX

FRAUD TRENDS

"The economic downturn has created the perfect storm as far as fraud is concerned." [40]

Fraud is an ancient problem, perhaps the world's second-oldest profession, we often joke around the office.

But like any phenomenon, it experiences cycles and trends. Knowing what's happening in the overall world of employee fraud can be extremely helpful when addressing your own fraud challenges. The most obvious trend to watch is the amount of fraud, since *a rising tide defrauds all banks.*[41] But there are also other trends to watch, such as the types of fraud, the types of fraudsters at work, and the channels used to attack financial institutions. But to conclude the first half of *Insidious*, let's take a look at some of the latest trends, starting with the scale of the problem.

Trend: Fraud really is on the rise

Among his many responsibilities, our colleague David Hood compiles an ongoing list of fraud incidents highlighted in print and on the web.[42] David—a soft-spoken father of two who looks a little like a cross between a long-distance runner and a cop—has been doing this for the last year or so. Lately, his email updates have seemed longer. In fact, they're clogging our inbox. The alleged fraud incidents described are larger. And the diversity of the schemes—particularly the employee schemes—is remarkable.

---

[40] "Managing Fraud in a Downturn," Special Report Publishing, *The Daily Telegraph* (UK), May 18, 2009.

[41] A rising tide actually floats all boats. But we're talking about banking, not boating. And more fraud in general means more fraud in specific—e.g., within your institution.

[42] You'll find his listings on our blog at www.bankfraudforum.com.

Consider these recent listings:

Former Iowa Bank Employee Pleads Guilty to Fraud
A former employee of Sac City Bank has pleaded guilty to defrauding customers out of $4 million. Forty-eight-year-old Charlene Pickhinke pleaded guilty Thursday in U.S. District Court in Sioux City to wire fraud, making a false statement in a bank's books and records, money laundering, and aggravated identity theft. (*Des Moines Register*, July 10, 2009)

Bank Fraud Conspirator Responsible for $100 Million in Bad Loans
Philip Coon awaits sentencing for his part in a scheme that skimmed proceeds from an extra point charged on mortgages issued by Coast Bank. Coon, who oversaw residential loans at Coast Bank, aggressively grew mortgages on homes that were mostly built by a sole developer who later claimed bankruptcy. The fraudulent dealings on the part of Coon contributed to the bank incurring more than $100 million in bad loans—some made to borrowers whose homes were never even started. (*Bradenton Herald*, June 27, 2009)

Former Minnesota Bank President Sentenced for Fraud
The former president and majority owner of First State Bank Minnesota in LeRoy, Minn., was sentenced Wednesday to 30 months in federal prison and ordered to pay $609,848 for misappropriating funds from the bank and its customers and for tax evasion. Gerald Alan Payne, 54, admitted to obtaining money from customer bank accounts, charging personal expenditures on the bank's credit cards and cashing checks written to the bank and others while keeping the cash for himself. (*Star Tribune*, May 13, 2009)

Bank Teller Charged with Fraud in $270,000 Scheme
A Bank of America teller was charged yesterday with fraud and accused
of participating in a scheme to steal about $270,000 from customers at
a branch in Peabody, according to the US attorney's office. Jeffrey C.
Gautreaux, 25, used his position to gain access to the accounts and personal
data of customers who had deposited funds at the bank. Gautreaux sold
account information to other people, who then used the information to
make unauthorized withdrawals from customers' accounts, according to
the indictment. (*The Boston Globe*, June 5, 2009)

Former Miami Beach Bank Manager Charged in $11 Million Fraud
Ricardo Figueredo, a former assistant bank manager of Bank of America and
Barnett Bank, was charged in federal court with bank fraud in a scheme to
misappropriate $11 million from customer accounts between the mid-1990s
and 2008. The prosecution alleges he misappropriated more than $11 million
in customer funds for personal investments in Guatemala, Spain and
elsewhere and used more than $1 million in customer funds "to support
his lavish lifestyle." (*Palm Beach Post*, January 22, 2009)

Former VP of Accounting Gets 2-year Sentence in Bank Fraud
A 62-year-old Omaha woman has been sentenced to two years in prison
and ordered to pay more than $786,000 in restitution. Federal prosecutors
say Caroline Domanski was vice president of accounting when she embezzled
about $1.4 million from First Nebraska Educators and Employees Group
Credit Union. Investigators say the theft occurred over a 15-year period
starting in 1993. (Action 3 News)

Former Branch Manager Sentenced—Total Loss: $20 Million
A former branch manager for Bank of America has been sentenced to 63
months in jail for his role in a $2 million fraud scheme. Oscar Sanchez took
bribes in return for opening fraudulent bank accounts and opening lines of
credit for the Khan Ring. The ring defaulted on loans and credit card debt,

causing millions in losses to numerous financial institutions, including Bank of America. Current loss estimates from the Khan Ring's fraudulent activities exceed $20 million. (U.S. Attorney, Southern District of New York)

These stories and hundreds more like them make us wonder—is employee fraud on the rise? Or is it simply in the news more often, thanks to the high-profile fraud cases of Société Générale and others? Or is our diligent colleague David just doing an exceptionally thorough job of finding fraud news?

Consider this quote from a recent UK special report on fraud.[43] "As pressure increases on us all financially, those employees who would not normally consider committing a fraud may be under enough pressure themselves to take the risk." Or these more quantifiable results from a recent survey of 500 fraud professionals:[44]

Employee fraud is the most rapidly growing type of fraud—48 percent of survey respondents indicated that employee embezzlement was on the rise, chosen over several other fraud categories.

Employee fraud is on the rise—More than half (55.4 percent) of respondents said that the level of fraud has slightly or significantly increased in the previous 12 months compared to the level of fraud they investigated or observed in years prior.

The pressure is on—About half (49.1 percent) of respondents cited increased financial pressure as the biggest factor contributing to the increase in fraud, compared to increased opportunity (27.1 percent) and increased rationalization (23.7 percent).

---

[43] "Managing Fraud in a Downturn," Special Report Publishing, *The Daily Telegraph* (UK), May 18, 2009.

[44] "Occupational Fraud: A Study of the Impact of an Economic Recession," Association of Certified Fraud Examiners, 2009. Note that this is a different, more focused report than the ACFE's bi-annual Report to the Nation, referenced in Chapter 4.

The internal controls are down—Nearly 60 percent of in-house fraud examiners reported that their companies had experienced layoffs during the past year. Among those who had experienced layoffs, almost 35 percent said their company had eliminated some controls.

The future looks fraud-filled—Nearly 90 percent of all respondents said they expect fraud to continue to increase during the next year. And the type of fraud they expect to increase most is employee embezzlement.

Now we can safely answer our own, often-asked question—*Is employee fraud on the rise?* The answer is *absolutely yes.* In addition to the study cited above, employee fraud consistently shows up on the top five concerns that banking CEOs have on their agendas. "Employee fraud is much more pervasive than the statistics show," concludes one industry veteran. "It's keeping a lot of bankers up at night. And it should. Because there's more of it than ever."

What are the reasons behind the rise?

An uncertain economy creates greater motivation and financial need among fraudsters. And it opens up new opportunities at organizations in transition or crisis, where internal controls are no longer doing their job. Or where employees just don't care about doing a great job anymore. A well-regarded industry pundit recently told us about her recent loan closing. "The closing was with a major financial institution with a name everyone would recognize, and it was a simple, conventional loan," she says. "I had provided all of the materials—I've done this several times before. And this time there were so many mistakes in the paperwork and in the process that it was unbelievable and outrageous. In the past, someone would have checked everything. Loan officers used to be conservative. Now they're on commission and more interested in volume than getting everything right. Mistakes and sloppy processes seem to be the norm now. And that just means more and more opportunities for someone to take advantage of the disarray."

There's big money in collusive fraud.

The result of marketplace turmoil? Revenue-sapping inefficiency and new opportunities for employee fraud.

Trend: Schemes are more sophisticated

Fraudsters exploit weaknesses. And new weaknesses open up new opportunities. More disgruntled, uncertain employees mean new recruits for fraud schemes. Which brings us to another trend, the use of employees as part of increasingly sophisticated schemes. "We're seeing a marked increase in the sophistication and complexity of employee schemes," says one trendwatcher. "And lots more internal-external schemes. Organized crime groups are recruiting or coercing people already within institutions, or planting people inside institutions. In a downturn, they're able to find more willing recruits among employees who are demoralized, convinced they're going to lose their jobs, or feeling tremendous financial pressure."

Within the trend toward sophisticated schemes, you'll find incredibly advanced technology used to defeat cyber-security efforts, fraud geniuses able to strike from afar (think Ukraine, Nigeria, and China) where fraud isn't as actively prosecuted, and long-developing schemes. Some sophisticated schemes (e.g., first-party, credit card bust-out) may smolder undetected for months, flame up and hit hard to register major dollar losses, then disappear. And employees help make these sophisticated schemes happen. Trusted insiders are the Most Valuable Players of fraud gangs.

Trend: Fraud is a team sport

The image of the fraudster as a disgruntled loner staying late to defraud his or her employer still applies to some fraudsters. But it's being supplanted by collusive teams that leverage insider information to gain a competitive advantage against fraud-detection technology and investigators.

We spent a lot of time considering all the various data types that can link seemingly unconnected individuals to reveal a fraud ring at work. It's really pretty fascinating. Shared addresses (IP, email, or physical), related Social Security Numbers, phone numbers, country of origin, similar account profiles and behaviors—these are just the beginning. Look into the finer details and the connections start to add up until collusive activity comes into focus. Visualized, the interconnections of collusive fraud start to look like the flight patterns between airports—except all that traffic leads to fraud damage and major dollar losses.

Collusive fraud generates higher losses and poses more risk to financial institutions. We know it's on the rise. And we see more and more insiders involved. Fraud is all about gangs now—the Khan Gang, Romanian web fraud gangs, global credit-card syndicates, 419 Fraud Gangs, Nigerian letter/email gangs, and more. Why? There's big money in collusive fraud. Fraudsters expand their operations for the same reasons that businesses expand—they have the capacity and differentiated skills to make more money. Plus, foreign rings target the U.S. because it's *where the money is*[45]—as well as the opportunities and vulnerabilities.

Safety in numbers

It's hard to track and shut down a complicated gang completely. Failure to identify the entire network often has an unintended side-effect—it emboldens the remaining members to do more damage. In many cases, *moles* or runners get caught, but rarely the kingpins or masterminds—who simply set up shop in new geographic areas. So in an era of more sophisticated fraud schemes and collusive gangs, financial institutions need even more vigilant monitoring, prevention, and investigation. And that means identifying the insiders who are enablers of, and active participants in, these schemes.

---

[45] Did you catch the Willie Sutton reference? He robbed banks because "that's where the money is."

Collusive fraud can stretch beyond one institution. "I'm seeing a lot more large ring cases," says Bill Perry, a fraud prevention and investigation veteran at Wachovia and a former FBI agent. "It's important to look at hundreds of cases and look at the patterns and groupings, trying to link cases together. Many times, these schemes cross banks, jurisdictions, and other boundaries. It's a major trend—and a real challenge for investigators and banks that aren't used to thinking big about fraud." Inside these rings, you'll find insiders with the knowledge of systems and controls (or lack thereof), access, and credibility necessary to enable the scheme to do the most damage.

Trend: Fraud crosses all products and channels

From a fraudster's perspective, cross-channel fraud makes perfect sense— exploiting multiple channels helps schemes grow and succeed. Plus, some delivery channels, such as online or telephone banking, are higher-risk channels than the branch network, where fraudsters encounter real people. Fraudsters exploit channels and their unique weaknesses and devolving controls. For example, wire transfers used to require a visit to a branch. Then they could be called in, but with call-back procedures and other mechanisms to mitigate risk. Now many large banks are moving toward realtime online wire origination.

So consider a fraudster who may buy account information from an insider, such as a teller. The fraudster can then use that information to perform account takeovers, taking out new loans, then ultimately using a near-instantaneous wire transfer to move his fraud funds out of the bank, where it is wired again and again, ultimately offshore. This simple example alone taps multiple delivery channels and shows how channels and their unique characteristics and weaknesses can be exploited.

Cross-channel fraud is on the rise because it enables sophisticated fraud schemes that generate higher losses (or gains, if you're thinking like a fraudster). And it exploits the tendency of banks to have siloed organizations, inconsistent internal controls, and detection systems that focus on one channel alone. Increasing products and channels increases opportunities for fraud—the news stories and experiential knowledge of fraud experts prove this trend out. But in terms of employee fraud, more channels means more potential insiders with access to them, and greater ability to help external fraud rings.

Cross-channel fraud opens up the playing field for fraud, by employees as well as outsiders. Secure one channel and you can see fraud jumping to other channels. And emerging channels, such as mobile, open up even more opportunities for fraud.

Trend: Limiting access

A related trend is that financial institutions are responding to the risks associated with access to multiple systems and channels. "We're seeing banks making a careful effort to limit access that employees have to systems," says Perry. "It used to be that everyone could pretty much access anything—that's what enabled great customer service. But it also opened up more opportunities for fraud, and more actual fraud. So prudent banks are carefully thinking through who needs access to what, and making managers justify the need for access." In short, trends like cross-channel fraud, which hinge on access to key banking systems and channels, have triggered new caution among banks looking to protect their organizations from unauthorized outside access, as well as misuse by trusted insiders. After all, at least the latter group is within their nominal control.

Somewhere, a disgruntled, stressed-out employee is sitting in a bank break room, beneath the fluorescent lights, thinking up a new fraud scheme right now.

Trend: Cultural acceptance of fraud

Start with pilloried bankers in the newspapers, portrayed as fat cats who deserve punishment and ridicule. Add outraged consumers. And then factor in a cultural admiration for sophisticated fraudsters.[46] What do you get? A complicated public relations challenge for banks, for one thing. But you also get a moral looseness and degraded sense of personal responsibility that can allow fraud to flourish within banks and among employees. After all, fraud rarely kills. It may destroy the life savings of a customer—but the bank covers that loss. So who is the real victim? Apply this kind of thinking to the personal level and you create an environment ripe with new motivations for (and justifications of) employee fraud. *They deserve it. No one cares. It's not a real crime.* These rationalizations go back to our earlier exploration of the core elements of employee fraud—opportunity and motivation. And it's clear that we're not exactly living in an era of zero tolerance for fraud.

Perhaps we can attribute it to fraud overload—too many mind-numbing stories in the media, too many staggering dollar losses, too many astounding data breaches. Or we can take a page from the culture wars and point to Hollywood as the villain, serving up handsome fraudsters (Clooney, Cage, *et al.*)[47] and thrilling scams that make old-style films like *Butch Cassidy and the Sundance Kid* and *The Thomas Crown Affair* look so very 20th century. Or we can even highlight generational differences, as in our last, related trend.

---

[46] Consider Frank Abagnale, the check fraudster who inspired the film *Catch Me If You Can*.

[47] Even Jérôme Kerviel of Société Générale fame/infamy has become a kind of counter-culture hero.

Trend: A more fraud-friendly generation of employees

We don't want to discriminate against younger people. We have lots of honest, hard-working young colleagues, like David, our fraud-finding friend mentioned at the beginning of this chapter. But to be honest, many of the experts we talked to recently about trends in employee fraud raised generational issues—albeit uncomfortably and with a great deal of caution. Their concerns start with technical skills. Younger employees are more computer and technology savvy than ever. And inherently more risky. Consider the Pfizer employee, who used a company laptop to download peer-to-peer software to share music videos. This software left the company open to access and exposed personal data of 17,000 former and current Pfizer employees to theft—triggering lawsuits and a public black eye.[48] Turned to the dark side (i.e., when a young tech-minded employee becomes a devious fraudster), these technological adepts are able to do more damage and exploit organizational weaknesses more completely.

Concerns about a fraud-friendly generation also focus on moral gray areas. A generation used to illegal file sharing and other online deceit isn't likely to be Aristotelian about right and wrong. Black and white is replaced by gray.

"Generation Y, the 20-somethings, just has a different attitude toward intellectual property," says Catherine Allen of the Santa Fe Group. "Put in a business context, this attitude can pose problems in the way employees view right and wrong. And that can have a real impact on the prevalence of employee fraud at all levels."

This trend may trigger an often-mentioned response—tighter regulation. "Increased regulation will have a real impact on creating a more ethical climate within banks," says one fraud investigator. "It can enforce accountability at all levels, from personal to organizational. And it can clean up the gray areas where fraud can be semi-justified by less-than-ethical employees of any age."

---

[48] Tim Wilson, "Tech Center: Insider Threat. Understanding the Danger Within," *Security Dark Reading/InformationWeek Analytics*, March 2009.

It's important to point out that despite widespread worries about younger employees, most fraud fighters acknowledge that the majority of employee fraudsters tend to be in their 30s to 40s—veteran employees and managers who are frustrated with their careers and able to rationalize stealing.

Turning knowledge into power

Knowing the trends can help banks do more than simply keep up to speed on the latest industry issues. By knowing what trends are afoot in employee fraud and related fraud schemes, banks can ensure that the fraud detection systems and processes they put into place address the key issues—such as cross-channel fraud and collusive gangs—that dominate industry events and publications. Today's trends inform tomorrow's solutions, ideally sooner rather than later. Because the one constant in employee fraud is change—new schemes emerge hourly. Somewhere, a disgruntled, stressed-out employee is sitting in a bank break room, beneath the fluorescent lights, thinking up a new fraud scheme right now—something brilliant and sophisticated, that delves deeply into systems no one really understands, and exploits internal controls that aren't strictly enforced.

Will your bank be able to detect and stop this nascent scheme and dozens others like it? We'll address that question in the second half of *Insidious*, where we move from exploring the complex problem of employee fraud to discussing what to do about it.

ENVISIONING A SOLUTION

CHAPTER SEVEN

NO SILVER
BULLET

"We can't solve problems by using the same kind
of thinking we used when we created them."

—Einstein

We've explored the problem of employee fraud and shown how it's insidious, expensive, complicated, and inherently human.

We've examined the trends and statistics and shown how employee fraud is growing. Now would generally be the time to start prescribing a solution. But we're not going to do that. Why not? Because any prescription would be simplistic and naive, since every bank is different—organizationally, culturally, and in terms of readiness for addressing employee fraud. Plus, employee fraud is definitely not the kind of problem that's open to a *one size fits all* kind of solution.

We want to suggest a different approach, one that acknowledges the real challenges of employee fraud and proposes a workable solution.

The traditional approach isn't always the best approach

First, consider the shortcomings of the traditional prescription, the kind that you'll hear from a lot of very well-paid and generally well-intentioned consultants. Though consultants may state their case differently, it generally boils down to *take a careful look at your people, processes, and technology.*

As we begin talking about how to explore solutions without devolving into prescriptive panaceas, we found ourselves in a conundrum. Some of our colleagues were almost allergic to the *people, processes, and technology* framework that is usually applied to solutions for enterprise-level problems, from customer relationship management to fraud. Others were okay with it, though they recognized its limitations. So what was the best way to explore the various issues around addressing employee fraud without falling into the trap of proposing a solution that might not be truly effective? For the answer, we turned to our curmudgeonly source, Deep Vault.

"Don't make me laugh," he said in a decidedly unfunny way. *"People, processes, and technology* are for management consultants who like to have nice little PowerPoint-friendly presentations about solutions," he says. "It's the kind of approach anybody without a lot of vision always trots out," he says. "Kinda makes sense, since these are the three general areas that feed into almost any business problem. But it's like when a doctor tells you to take *two aspirin and call me in the morning.* It can't really hurt, but it's a perfunctory prescription at best, ineffective at worst. And it neatly avoids the complicating factors that keep companies from addressing employee fraud in a meaningful, effective way."

With this insight in mind, let's take a look at the traditional, three-pointed prescriptive approach and identify some of the issues that make it less than optimal.

First, you have to decide to address fraud

The prescriptive approach assumes that banks have made the decision to address employee fraud, which isn't always the case. There are plenty of reasons why banks might choose the status quo. It's easier, cheaper (in the short run), and some organizations are simply willing to accept egregious fraud incidents, losses, and risk of reputational damage as a cost of doing business. An institution that wants to address the problem has to start by moving from denying the existence (or importance) of the problem of employee fraud, to accepting it as an issue, to deciding to address it. It's the classic shock/denial/anger/acceptance[49] shift, applied to a very specific problem—employee fraud.

Addressing employee fraud doesn't mean stopping it completely. Stopping all employee fraud is an ideal, like stopping all traffic accidents. You can educate and inform the drivers (people), set speed limits and enforce the rules (processes/internal controls), and make the cars and roads better and safer (technology). But there are still going to be accidents (fraud events)—ideally, fewer though, and less severe. You want to avoid regular accidents, as well as the major pile-ups—the big fraud events that trigger high-dollar losses and put your bank in the headlines.

---

[49] Originally established by Kubler-Ross, and appropriated by almost every self-help program ever created.

But still, denial makes many banks assume that accidents won't happen, since they haven't had one yet. Or because they try to drive safely. Employee fraud happens, believe it.

Employees are people, not criminals (yet)

The inherently human nature of employee fraud doesn't lend itself to easy solutions, as we discussed previously, since it's difficult to predict which employees are going to commit fraud. "Employee fraud isn't the kind of problem that Human Resources departments can fend off by screening more carefully," says Bill Perry, Wachovia's fraud investigations veteran. "Though banks should always be checking all of the internal and external *don't hire* lists to weed out people with criminal backgrounds, the real problems happen after people join the company. And there's no way to spot potential fraudsters—such as people who, under the right circumstances, are going to be willing to break the rules for their own gain. Or worse, people without consciences. Unfortunately, you can't see that just by looking someone in the eyes. If we could, there wouldn't be any fraud, or crime for that matter."

In general, employee fraud doesn't happen because banks are hiring criminals. They're hiring people. Then when people are confronted by the potentially seductive and dangerous combination of opportunity and motivation,[50] they can become fraudsters—not all of them, of course, just a small but damaging subset of the overall employee population. It's safe to say that it would be almost impossible to tell, from initial hiring checks, if a new-hire is going to go to the dark side and start stealing—particularly when employee fraud can happen at any level in an organization, from CSRs to CEOs.

---

[50] Opportunity (covered in Chapter 1) gives bank employees access to systems that enable fraud. Motivation (covered in Chapter 2) pushes normal, honest employees to become fraudsters—often for completely understandable reasons.

At larger institutions, the sheer volume of incoming employees creates another complicating factor in addressing the *people* angle of employee fraud. Banks are retail organizations that rely on a steady flow of entry-level employees. Clearly, making careful hiring decisions is important to the ability to provide excellent customer service and ensure the overall health of a customer-centric organization. But implementing draconian hiring practices can trigger problems filling key slots, slow the steady flow of entry-level employees, and encourage candidates to apply elsewhere. In short, you can create operational problems by trying to hire your way out of an employee fraud problem.

Processes and internal controls are only as good as their enforcement
Next we move to the second area often highlighted as critical to addressing employee fraud—*processes*, or internal controls. All financial institutions have internal controls and processes of various degrees of strictness. However, simply having strong internal controls isn't enough—they have to be followed and enforced, otherwise, they're not an effective deterrent to employee misbehavior and fraud. Enron was known for having extremely strong and well-documented internal controls. But clearly, these controls weren't enforced—or were enforced erratically throughout the organization. The same laxness is behind the many high-profile control lapses at major financial institutions.

Or consider drug testing in baseball. It's a great example of controls that were weak, poorly enforced, and actually allowed ball players to get away with taking steroids. No matter what the industry or organization, it's clear that internal controls are very hard to enforce consistently.

Why controls are a challenge
There are many reasons why good-intentioned internal controls wind up being ineffective. During times of organizational turmoil—layoffs, mergers, and other changes—internal controls often fall by the wayside, particularly the time-consuming controls. Managers have more pressing challenges and problems, so they quit enforcing the processes and routines that can catch fraud, such as

surprise teller audits. The person in charge of oversight or implementing controls can end up leaving the company or getting laid off thanks to a downsizing or merger. They can simply become negligent because of low morale or waning commitment to the company. Controls can start affecting customer service, and get bypassed in the interest of better service. And in times of heady growth when all seems well, managers are less motivated to look for potential problems.

Fraudsters take advantage of the trust of co-workers

There's another enemy of internal controls—*trust*. As groups work together over the years, they fall into informal ways of working and collaborating, routines that probably don't comply completely with internal control policies. Managers let their staffs know about upcoming surprise audits or cash counts, defeating their purpose and eliminating any chance of catching fraud. They let employees go beyond established approval limits, creating the opportunity for higher fraud losses.

Over time, workers become aware of internal controls, and devise ways to defeat them. For example, one bank we visited recently was monitoring General Ledger transactions over $500 exclusively. The result? A remarkable number of fraudulent transactions just below that $500 threshold.

Creating a fraud-ready climate

Any reduction or undermining of internal controls opens up new opportunities for fraud. An organization that isn't enforcing its internal controls is like a homeowner who leaves all the doors unlocked, cancels the insurance policy, and puts a sign out front asking thieves to come on in. As the saying goes, "The true test of a person's character is how he or she behaves when no one is watching." Ineffective internal controls put every employee's character to the test by creating a climate where *no one is watching*—and many find that they're capable of committing fraud, explained away by the usual justifications.[51]

---

[51] "I was going to repay the money. I deserve the money. No one will miss it. The company owes me." And many more...

"We have to accept that employee fraud isn't going to be stopped by processes and internal controls."

Keeping an eye on the CSRs, not the SVPs

Another issue with internal controls is that they are generally biased toward lower-level employees. "The fact is that lower-level employees have plenty of internal controls, while higher-ups have fewer," says one former banking executive with decades of fraud experience. Controls tend to keep an eye on lower-level workers (CSRs, tellers, operations clerks, and others throughout the organization). Statistically, there are more people (and potential fraudsters) at this level, given the low-rise pyramid structure of most financial services org charts. However the truly jaw-dropping fraud losses are generally caused by trusted executives at the branch manager level or above.[52] "Here's the problem —people defer to employees with experience and rank and give them higher approval levels without going to the loan committee or getting other approvals," says our banking executive. "This completely understandable tendency lets executives get away with huge frauds."

She concludes with a great phrase that says it all: "We have to accept that employee fraud isn't going to be stopped by processes and internal controls," she says, not with an air of dejection, but an honest appraisal of reality. "With tens of thousands of employees, you simply cannot monitor everyone and everything all the time."

---

[52] Higher ranking employees mean higher losses.

Investing in technology

Last but definitely not least, we need to consider the role of technology in enabling financial institutions to address employee fraud. Technology is frequently invoked as a panacea for all problems—organizational, economic, environmental, and more. Technology is often invoked as a cure-all, and for good reason—in addition to promising near-magical results,[53] it removes humans from responsibility, partially or completely. For our purposes and context, let's define technology to include advanced monitoring and detection, other automated methods of identifying employee fraud, and forensic investigations. Even within this relatively narrow definition of technological solutions, there is wide variance in the cost, size, underlying technology, implementation complexity, organizational impact, and (most importantly) effectiveness. As any technology-savvy executive knows, investing in technology isn't necessarily an answer—it's often just an expense. Or it could achieve great results.

The key point is that technology is not a silver bullet either. It needs to be carefully selected and implemented to achieve its ultimate goal—detecting and ultimately reducing employee fraud. And it has to have the ability to be accurate at detecting fraud as well as flexible enough to change rapidly with the ever-evolving challenges of employee fraud.

Examining data, empowering experts

So if the traditional *people, processes, and technology* represent a simplistic, broad-spectrum prescription, what's the alternative? Fortunately, employee fraud is not an intractable, unsolvable problem. There is a new way forward, one that lets your institution take advantage of the two key fraud-fighting resources that it already has—data and experts. We don't think of it as a prescription. Let's simply call it an approach, one that's available to any financial institution that recognizes that employee fraud is a problem and decides to address it.

---

[53] "Any sufficiently advanced technology is indistinguishable from magic," Arthur C. Clark.

Data can be a goldmine in the fight against fraud. And your bank already owns the mine and the gold.

Yes, employee fraud is a daunting problem, more of a disease than an injury. But within the disease resides an element of the cure—in much the same way that vaccines are often derived from the deadly virus itself. This critical element gives banks a weapon (though not a silver bullet) when fighting employee fraud. That weapon is data.

Every employee action leaves *digital bread crumbs* along a trail that is clear and unique. These patterns, if detected, can lead investigators to fraud. They can be obscured within the sheer volume of data. But they're there, awaiting discovery, investigation, and interpretation. Then this newly gained knowledge can be turned into an antidote for similar future fraud by spotting the same patterns of behavior that indicate the presence of fraud.

Data also enables banks to spot outlier behaviors—actions that indicate something highly unusual is happening that appears to be suspicious. This data is invaluable in identifying potential fraud.

In short, data can be a goldmine in the fight against fraud. And your bank already owns the mine and the gold. It's simply a matter of finding the evidence of fraud, which becomes a much more focused challenge—one that we explore in more detail in the next chapter.

People have the power

But data is just one element of addressing employee fraud. Your organization already has another significant weapon against employee fraud—the experienced fraud fighters who analyze data and investigate cases. These skilled, committed personnel know your organization, its systems, and its vulnerabilities. Supplying analysts and investigators with powerful tools to find more fraud, more easily can make a major difference in the fight against fraud. We'll talk to analysts and investigators, and explore the two interrelated capabilities that they bring—detection and investigation—in Chapter 9.

So while there is no silver bullet to fight fraud, there are certainly weapons, tools, strategies, and solutions that generate real results. And that's good news for banks that choose to address the insidious problem of employee fraud.

CHAPTER EIGHT

ALL FRAUD LEAVES EVIDENCE BEHIND

"Intuition becomes increasingly valuable in the new information society precisely because there is so much data."

—John Naisbitt

Employee fraud is a crime that creates its own evidence in the form of data.

In the end, no matter how it's committed, or who does the stealing—from customer service representatives to chief executive officers—employee fraud requires interacting with a financial institution's applications and systems, including the General Ledger, core banking systems, and CRM systems. These interactions create records, data, and evidence. Think of it as *electronic fingerprints.*

Data is a critical weapon in the fight to detect and stop employee fraud. It provides the evidence of employees taking inappropriate actions that indicate potential fraud, from account look-ups to transfers of funds to suspicious credits. Your transaction systems serve as a camera, capturing specific evidence of fraud within the vast landscape of data.

In short, all fraud creates data, which is very good news for banks. But data—and how it's stored, managed, accessed, organized, and searched—also raises some of the most difficult challenges in mitigating employee fraud. Fortunately, there are solutions that help turn data from a daunting challenge to the core of an effective fraud-detection system. But they require a new approach.

Leveraging data to fight fraud

Even smaller financial institutions have millions of data fields, while larger ones have mind-numbing amounts of data. Because of the transaction-based structure of financial services—as well as strict regulations on record-keeping—every action taken on a customer account, internal account, or other system creates an audit trail that documents that action. In the end, this data may reside within transactional systems, relational databases, or other storage mechanisms.

Simply having a lot of data doesn't mean you can find fraud. In a similar way, simply having a lot of assets doesn't mean a financial institution knows how to generate an impressive return. It's what you do with the data that counts.

Consulting the experts

Our colleague Greg Leibon speaks very eloquently about how lofty mathematical theory intersects with the much more prosaic work of finding employee fraud. Now our chief mathematician, Greg's also a professor at Dartmouth whose research focuses on topology, probability, and pattern recognition. To give you an idea of the complexity of Greg's work, consider this abstract of a paper he presented at a recent International Conference on Symbolic and Algebraic Computation:

A Fast Hermite Transform with Applications to Protein Structure Determination

We discuss algorithms for a fast and stable approximation of the Hermite transform of a compactly supported function on the real line, attainable via an application of a fast algebraic algorithm for computing sums associated to a three-term relation. Trade-offs between approximation in bandwidth (in the Hermite sense) and size of the support region are addressed. Generalizations to any family of orthogonal polynomials are outlined. Applications to the determination of protein structure are discussed.

Ouch. And we were still recovering from his "Delaunay Triangulations and Voronoi Diagrams for Riemannian Manifolds." Luckily, Greg is also an extremely nice guy who lives in Vermont, who wears his hair pulled back in a ponytail, and who can talk to mere mortals about complex mathematical concepts in an enlightening and understandable way.

"I love working with non-mathematicians," he says. "I like walking into business situations and working with experts to solve problems no one else could solve—like finding fraud in an ocean of data." So how does he do that? "Understanding fraud requires working closely with experts who know the problem well, then translating that understanding into new ways to monitor for fraud. Identifying fraud isn't a purely mathematical challenge. It's a business challenge—and an intrinsically human one. But at the core, you have data to examine."

Modeling behaviors

We talked to Greg recently about the specific data challenges involved in finding employee fraud, rather than external fraud, such as credit card fraud or check fraud. The first challenge he mentioned is the high impact and the relative rarity of employee fraud. "Employee fraud can trigger big losses, but statistically, it's a relatively rare occurrence—certainly more rare than a widespread external fraud like credit card fraud—so you have to go through a lot of data to find it," he says. "The good news is that you have a lot of data to work with. But if you find evidence of fraud in the data, that means the fraud has already been perpetrated, which is problematic from a loss perspective. So what you really want to do is model the employee behaviors that lead to fraud, then identify those behaviors. That way you can monitor for fraud *before it happens*, look for vulnerabilities, and truly protect banks." In short, Greg quickly turned a discussion about *detection* into one focused on *protection*.

Greg points out how the rich data that banks have at their fingertips (or at least within reach) is essential in modeling these behaviors. "Consider teller fraud," he says. "Banks have a lot of tellers. They log onto systems that capture a huge chunk of their day in data. This data lets you see typical and atypical behavior over the huge number of employee actions."

Unusual activity isn't always fraud

But simply spotting *different* behaviors isn't going to identify fraud. It's simply going to identify mathematical outliers—people who are doing certain actions differently. Many of these differences have rational explanations that do not involve fraud. A teller may work in a non-standard way, may have a unique customer base, or may simply be different, though not necessarily a fraudster.

"Behaviors vary a great deal even with a peer group like tellers," he says. "Unusual behaviors may be worth looking at, but they don't necessarily mean fraud. And if you simply identify different behavior, you're going to wind up generating a lot of false positives." And false positives waste valuable time and distract companies from identifying real fraud.

Context means everything

How can you move beyond identifying differences to identifying fraud? A key part of the answer is *contextualization*. "Context is crucial when you're talking about employee fraud," says Greg. "You have to make sure you're comparing apples to apples. Even peer groups like tellers are diverse. You have tellers in big city locations and small-town branches. You have experienced and inexperienced tellers. Actions which might seem normal in one context aren't in another."

Contextualization often starts with revisiting *assigned peer groups*, which are based on the programmatic job codes issued by Human Resources. Instead, it's important to establish *natural peer groups* to examine employee actions in context. Identifying these groups requires detailed knowledge about the specific operations of a bank or credit union—the details that make every financial institution unique. So while fraud detection systems can spot differences, *context* helps ensure that these differences are meaningful.

The challenges of context

"Context can be pretty subtle," says Greg. "You need to consider geographical context, since people behave differently in different parts of the country. You need to explore demographic context, since the customers banks serve also have a major impact. For example, a bank serving an elderly population may have a lot of account look-ups, since this population tends to call up and ask to verify information. Knowing these differences is all part of contextualization. And it requires systems flexible enough to be adjusted and fine tuned to recognize context and limit peer groups."

But narrowing down peer groups has its limits, expressed in the decidedly mathematical term *variance bias trade-off*. "What this term means is that if the peer group is too small, you don't have enough data. But if the peer group is too big, the results are biased because you're lumping people together who don't belong together." The key is to find groups of the right size to examine, then ensure that their actions are evaluated in context. Establishing accurate peer groups from the start enables fraud detection systems to measure variance, spot outliers accurately, model those behaviors that indicate fraud, and protect your institution and customers against employee fraudsters.

Lonely at the top

Greg also highlights an issue we've raised earlier—the organizational structure of most financial institutions means that there are a lot of tellers, customer service representatives, and others on the frontline of customer interaction, as well as the backrooms of bank operations. There is plenty of data on their actions. But at the higher levels, such as branch manager and above, the groups are smaller —as is the amount of data that can be examined. "Fraud by lower-level employees leaves coherent, first-order signatures within the data," he says. "Finding fraud gets harder and more complex as you move up the organization. That's where you need to envision likely fraud scenarios—the activities that a higher-level person might take if they are committing fraud—and apply them to the group you're monitoring."

"Fraud by lower-level employees leaves coherent, first-order signatures within the data."

These scenarios might be driven by experience, such as fraud that happened in the past or that seems likely. We call this *the fraud you know*. Or they might be triggered by insights gleaned from examining employee behavior (at all levels in the organization) and identifying suspicious anomalies. This type of fraud is *the fraud you don't know*. Ideally, a fraud-detection solution should be capable of identifying both types of fraud, known scenarios and unknown schemes—as well as monitoring all levels of your organization proactively.

"By applying advanced analytics to the right data, you can spot people behaving strangely," says Greg. "And you can tailor the indicators to find fraud effectively."

The challenges raised by data

However, Greg is clear that examining data isn't always easy. "Unfortunately, most banking systems weren't designed with the intent of finding fraud," he says. "They were designed to handle transactions efficiently. It's just not as simple as collecting all the logged data and combing through it. From a data point of view, the timing and order of various sequences is critical when looking for fraud. But few banks have a sensible, clean data set where you can go to find fraud."

The challenges? The data sets are huge, so they can be difficult to manage. There are often multiple systems creating transaction data, but structuring it in different ways. So a significant amount of data housekeeping is often required before arriving at a data set that can be examined, analyzed, and searched. And this housekeeping isn't simply about numbers—it requires a lot of knowledge about how the specific bank works, and records data.

"You want the data files to collide together in a precise way that provides a clear, sequential, account-level view that helps bring fraud to light," he concludes. "But it can take a lot of preliminary work to get the data in shape."

Managing data is a key element of solving fraud

Our colleagues spend a fair amount of time doing exactly that, and we can attest that it's painstaking work, particularly since every bank is unique in the way it records and handles data. But in the end, it's worth it. Data is at the foundation of the effort to address the problem of employee fraud. The ability to parse, manage, search, and analyze this data provides a powerful tool for detecting fraud, and protecting your organization. This work is handled by advanced fraud detection systems capable of working with massive amounts of data more effectively and automatically than humanly possible. But data alone is only part of the answer.

The human touch

As Greg points out, creating an effective solution requires the expertise of people with deep domain knowledge about the organization—who should be tapped with establishing and implementing your fraud detection solution. The importance of human expertise continues once the system is up and running, bringing us to the second component of the approach we proposed in the last chapter. The expertise comes in the form of key personnel within your organization—fraud analysts and fraud investigators. We'll meet these key groups—and explore their unique needs—in the next chapter.

CHAPTER NINE

DETECTION AND INVESTIGATION

"There are two sides to every question."

—Protagoras

We think of the two sides of addressing employee fraud as fraud *detection* and *investigation*.

They're different but interrelated capabilities. They're often handled by separate groups within an organization, who perform different tasks that tap job-specific skills. In the end, though, you need to integrate both detection and investigation to protect your enterprise from employee fraud. Here we'll take a closer look at each of these two critical capabilities, the people behind them, and the challenges they face.

The machinery of fighting fraud has two key parts

When addressing the challenges of employee fraud, it helps to break down this abstract, monolithic idea into smaller, more operational pieces, such as detection and investigation. To begin, consider the ultimate goal of each capability, reduced to its simplest level. Fraud detection helps protect your organization from losses by identifying possible fraud early and accurately. Fraud investigation identifies and investigates fraud events, brings fraudsters to justice, and attempts to recover funds to the fullest extent possible. Think of these two capabilities as the yin/yang of employee fraud—both elements have to integrate seamlessly to form an enterprise approach to managing and reducing fraud. Both capabilities thrive on collaboration among experts. And doing both well is important to catching more fraud, more often and earlier—reducing fraud, avoiding potential reputational damage, and recovering stolen funds.

Fraud detection—monitoring and more

Fraud detection comes first in the continuum. At a high level, it involves any activity that helps identify unusual and potentially fraudulent employee activities or behavior—from installing video cameras trained on tellers to implementing monitoring systems to identify fraud scenarios. Detection comes in two types— *proactive detection* spots fraud before losses occur while *reactive detection* helps uncover a fraud scheme before it expands, spreads, and creates higher losses.

Proactive detection is about vigilance and prevention. It's like an alarm system that alerts you when someone breaks a window in your house. It can even serve as a deterrent, stopping thieves from breaking that window because they see the alarm company's sticker on it. Proactive detection identifies fraud prior to a loss occurring or becoming significant—and before money leaves the bank, which we refer to as the *point of value transfer*.

Reactive detection is about responsiveness and speed. It comes into play when the police respond to your alarm and chase the thieves *after* they make off with all your valuables. Reactive detection can result from a customer complaint, an employee call to a hotline, or early evidence of fraud. It can help detect interconnected fraud, or discover that fraudsters were responsible for other unexplained, different, but costly crimes.

In a perfect world, proactive detection would be enough. You would catch any possible unusual behavior right when it happens, and before any real damage is done. Unfortunately, financial institutions are too complicated for that. There are too many people doing too many tasks on too many diverse systems to rely solely on proactive detection. And fraudsters are often ahead of detection techniques. Plus, many types of fraud mimic honest, legitimate behavior. So success requires a blend of proactive and reactive fraud prevention processes. Your institution has to be able to react quickly to early indicators of fraud, fending off larger losses. Some fraudsters tend to start small with initial schemes (putting the proverbial toe in the water), so it's best to be able to react as quickly as possible. Others may steal large amounts of money immediately from a customer account, or via loan fraud. In these cases, fast reaction can determine how much of these funds are recovered.

"We look for suspicious alerts that indicate common events across our company," says a Wachovia analyst. "Then we work to shut them down quickly. The longer an event goes on, the more the losses creep up. So while we like to catch more fraud proactively, we also know that we have to react quickly to fraud that's already underway."

All about alerts and analysts

Ultimately, most employee fraud requires some activity that may appear completely normal, but isn't when examined in the context of a peer group (e.g., one teller performing hundreds of account look-ups during a shift while other tellers made only a few). Proactive detection systems can identify anomalies, policy violations, and other suspicious activities, then issue automatic *alerts*. Analysts evaluate these alerts for evidence of fraud, relying on analytic and investigative tools, as well as their own experience and expertise. In this way, detecting fraud is as much about *art* as *science*.

Organizationally, banks may make the Loss Prevention group part of Audit, Operations, or other areas—depending on the size of the organization and how it's structured. No matter where they fit on the organizational chart, *loss prevention analysts* (or just *analysts*) bring critical, specialized skills to the challenges of detection.

"A good analyst has accurate, intuitive gut feelings about alerts—and whether they indicate real fraud," says one career fraud-fighter from a major bank. "It's important to point out that all alerts aren't necessarily indicative of fraud —there's often a perfectly good reason for the anomaly. Analysts have to know what it is." In short, analysts add an interpretive, *human* element that helps separate actionable alerts (those likely to indicate fraud) and false positives (the inevitable but unwanted alerts that can be explained).

Portrait of an analyst

What are analysts like? Their title says it all—they're analytic. They're experts at analyzing alerts from fraud detection systems, as well as other information (e.g., customer and account data). They're deft at pulling all the data together—from the teller journals, customer accounts, General Ledger accounts, and more, then interpreting it in ways that go beyond simple evaluation. They rely on a range of analysis tools (some internal, others off-the-shelf, still others integrated with the fraud detection system).

Temperamentally, analysts are detail-oriented, focused, and generally pretty serious—which is good, because their daily work is challenging and important. They may feel a little under-appreciated, since their work is largely invisible when all goes well, becoming all-too-visible when it doesn't (e.g., when they miss evidence of employee fraud that turns into a big loss). They could be the air traffic controllers of fraud.

More than likely, they started in another area of the bank, and are leveraging deep knowledge of the organization, its products and its systems. Outside hires rarely start as employee fraud analysts—banks are too diverse and heterogeneous to make fraud analysis, particularly fraud involving employees, a commodity skill.

The value of their work is often measured in loss avoidance, a difficult-to-estimate number. That said, they take great pride in their work and are passionate about finding fraud.

Finding actionable alerts

Depending on the size of the bank, analysts may receive dozens or hundreds of alerts a day—generated by whatever fraud detection systems and protocols the bank has in place. The detection system could be an in-house system, a third-party system, or a combination or systems.[54] The analyst serves as the first reviewer of these alerts, and must quickly determine which ones merit further exploration, and which do not (false positives). False positives are an inherent byproduct of any automated monitoring system, but they must be kept as low as possible, since they waste the valuable time of analysts, and can obscure real fraud.

So analysts are under pressure to do a lot quickly. They have to process lots of alerts and make quick dispositions—all without missing a meaningful alert that leads to a stomach-dropping fraud (and that lands them in hot water). Sound hard? It is.

---

[54] We'll talk more about these systems in the next chapter.

Fraud investigation: different but just as important

Another aspect of enterprise fraud management is fraud investigation, which identifies fraudsters and helps recover losses.

Investigation picks up where analysis lets up—ideally as seamlessly as possible. Analysts deliver actionable internal fraud alerts to investigators, who then dig into the case, investigating it from all angles. The work of investigators covers:

additional forensic [55] research to determine whether an employee interview is warranted

coordination with other internal departments (HR, Legal, Audit)

management of a large case load, completing required forms, such as Suspicious Activity Reports (SARs) and other documents, and

working with law enforcement, as appropriate.

Organizationally, the Fraud Investigation group can be in Enterprise Fraud Management or part of the Corporate Security division. However, in smaller organizations, fraud analysts and fraud investigators may be part of the same group, and may be part of Operations, Security, or Audit. In exceptionally small institutions, the analyst and investigator may be the same person.

Fraud investigators at a glance

Fraud investigators tend to be former law enforcement officers of some capacity (FBI, local law enforcement, military) or have a degree in Criminal Justice. And they bring a different set of skills to the table than analysts.

---

[55] In this use, *forensic* doesn't imply the fingernail and hair sample forensics of CSI and other crime-scene shows, but goes back to the true definition of forensic—*applying scientific methods and techniques to the investigation of crime.* (Oxford American Dictionary, 2006)

"Effective case management is about making quick, good decisions about alerts and cases. With strong data management and integration, analysts and investigators can easily access relevant information and bring together critical evidence for forensic investigations. The result is a tight link between fraud detection, investigation, and reaction."

—Avivah Litan, Distinguished Analyst, Gartner Inc.

Maybe it's because they've seen other, more visceral crimes than employee fraud (the kind that leave bloodstains on floors, not on balance sheets), but investigators have a certain *attitude* when dealing with employee fraud—one that reveals knowledge of human behavior that extends well beyond bank lobbies and meeting rooms. In short, investigators know that even good people are capable of committing crimes. They know that every case is different (*case by case basis* is a catch-phrase of investigators) and are slow to generalize. And they take their work very seriously.

What do investigators like?

They like a case they can sink their teeth into—one with lots of facts and details. They like analysts who will work with them to locate additional layers of evidence and related facts or monitor evolving situations. They like to be able to get to the data they need to *work the case*—quickly and easily. And they like to have tools available to them that make the daunting work of case management simpler. After all, investigators may be working dozens of cases at any given time.

What don't they like? False positives, bureaucracy, waiting for data, and allowing fraudsters an opportunity to get away with fraud. In short, they want to catch the bad guys (and girls), get the money back, and get bad employees out of the company. They also like to prosecute and put fraudsters behind bars whenever possible.

Confessions and confrontations

Investigators who deal with employee fraud tend to be in a separate group from investigators working on external fraud challenges (e.g., credit card fraud perpetrated exclusively by an outside ring). The legal issues around investigating employees are significant and sophisticated, and require a very diplomatic approach, to say the least—just ask anyone in Human Resources. Banks often balance investigating internal fraud vigorously with the risk of exposing the organization to costly and distracting lawsuits.

Eventually the work of an investigator builds up enough evidence of fraud to confront the employee. This key event can mean the difference between getting a confession or providing early warning to fraudsters to shut down their nascent scheme or evolve it into another scheme. So investigators are careful to have all their facts in place, to move ahead at the right time, and to do whatever they can to recover funds that have left the bank (ideally, temporarily).

Leaving investigation to professionals

These interrogations, though they stop far short of waterboarding, can still be disturbing. For example, we spoke to a bank manager the other day who ended up getting drafted into confronting a fraudster in her bank, since an investigator wasn't available to come to her remote branch. Though the event happened almost twenty years ago, her memory of it was clear, disturbing, and raw.

"She was a teller everyone knew and liked, and she did something really stupid —she took some money out of her drawer. I think it was $20 or so," our friend recalls, extremely tentatively, when we ask her to recount her first and only employee fraud interview. "I confronted her and she confessed and started to cry. I had to have her write out a confession in my office, and she was crying the whole time. I'm sure she intended to pay the money back. And I'm sure she would have. But in the end, we had to fire her," she says, then issues the clincher. "If she had asked me to loan her $20, I would have. I really would have. So the whole incident never even had to happen."

But it did happen. And even though $20 is an unusually low dollar-loss, this particularly poignant anecdote points out why employee confrontations are left to investigators, who know how to get confessions while sidestepping the messy emotionality. Make no mistake about it, investigators have empathy for employees who steal, to a point. But they also see fraudsters for what they really are— thieves who are stealing from their unsuspecting and benevolent employers.

Getting to "I did it!"

Investigators employ a variety of interrogation techniques. "We might start by flattering them and telling them how impressive their scheme was," recalls a former investigator. "We might confront them with a stack of evidence and tell them the game is over. Or we might play hardball, to whatever degree is ethically allowable. We choose the tactics on a case by case basis." [56]

The reaction? Tears, confessions, denial, excuses, silence, vomiting, and more— none of it very pretty to watch, even for pros.

---

[56] We mentioned earlier that investigators like this phrase. And here it is.

"Sometimes, it's almost like a relief when they know they've been caught," our investigator says. "It's like they've been under enormous pressure to hide their stealing, and now they can let it go. Looking at the good side, we're giving them a chance to confess and move on."

Every fruitful investigation triggers a Suspicious Activity Report (SAR) filing. Banks file these reports with The Financial Crimes Enforcement Network (FinCEN), a division of the Department of the Treasury, which shares them with law enforcement. When someone commits fraud, it shows up on their permanent record, potentially ruining their career in banking. So investigators take their work very seriously, and protect the innocent when they come under scrutiny erroneously. That said, they want to remove the proverbial bad apples.

Following the money

Ultimately, banks don't want confessions or excuses. They want their money back. The result of an investigation might resolve internally, with the employee paying back some (ideally, all) of the stolen funds. Or investigators may work with law enforcement to build a case against an employee and pursue restitution via the courts. The goal is the same—to get back as much of the institution's money as possible. Recovering losses is the bottom line for investigators—it's what their work is measured by, whether those losses are generated by internal or external fraudsters.

Detection and investigation: the issues

So far, our discussion has focused on the specific responsibilities of these two key groups—analysts and investigators. In an ideal world, these groups work together seamlessly, sharing information and working toward common goals. This collaboration is even more important on internal fraud, as opposed to external fraud, where their work is more separate. There can be competition (of the healthy variety) but the focus should be on collaboration. For example, there should be a tight feedback loop that directs the findings of investigators back to the detection work of analysts. What investigators are finding at the end

There should be a tight feedback loop that directs the findings of investigators back to the detection work of analysts.

of the process should inform what analysts are looking for at the beginning. In this way, enterprise fraud management can respond to ever-evolving schemes.

Unfortunately, many analysts and investigators don't have adequate tools to enable a high level of collaboration. Too often during our discussions with banks we find that analysts are struggling to stay afloat in an ocean of false positives —triggering efficiency issues, raising frustration, and lowering morale.

In terms of data, we find that accessing core data (where fraud evidence often resides) can be difficult and time-consuming. Plus, lack of a comprehensive, enterprise-wide view of data prohibits analysis and investigation of cross-channel fraud schemes. From a collaboration perspective, we find major investigative limitations created by technical constraints, foremost among them, a lack of a common solution for analysts and investigators. Separate systems for alert management and case management make it difficult to make quick, well-informed, collaborative decisions.

We also find that many investigators, despite their skills and best intentions, need more powerful, more comprehensive case management capabilities (e.g., forensic research) that go beyond traditional systems—the kind of tools that enable them to uncover unknown, interconnected fraud, build bulletproof cases, and maximize financial recovery.

Making a case for better fraud management

The net result of technical limitations is slow, incomplete investigations. And banks often fail to identify sophisticated schemes, such as collusive fraud (employees and outsiders), and cross-channel schemes. If they are able to identify them, it's often the result of tedious, painstaking, and time-consuming manual effort. And in the end, they really can't be sure they have identified all the parties involved.

And these issues are only the beginning. If you ever wonder whether your organization has the tools and support it needs to fight employee fraud, or if you need to make a case for justifying investment in these tools, take a refreshingly simple step—ask your analysts and investigators. More than likely, you'll get an earful. Because despite their many differences, analysts and investigators share a common quality (not shared by fraudsters)—they tend to be brutally honest.

CHAPTER TEN

ESSENTIAL QUALITIES

"Fast is fine, but accuracy is everything."

—Xenophon

We have made it clear that we do not intend to prescribe a specific solution to employee fraud.

Why? Every financial institution is different—with varying levels of risk and preparedness, as well as a unique infrastructure, corporate culture, and specific internal controls. Without deep knowledge of your financial institution, pre-scribed solutions are perfunctory. So we'll leave the prescriptions to physicians and pharmacists.

That said, rising above the solution level, there are some key qualities that are essential to the success of any solution that you choose to implement to protect your financial institution from employee fraud. Taking a broad view helps you focus on the truly essential qualities—accuracy, speed, and flexibility—as well as secondary qualities that are also critical for fighting fraud.

In all, these qualities give you a clear context for evaluating your current solution for protecting your organization from employee fraud, as well as any new solution you might consider. And by solution, we're not simply focused on technology, since an effective solution encompasses broader measures—from creating an anti-fraud culture to implementing effective controls and processes. However, these qualities also hold true when looking specifically at enterprise fraud detection technologies.

The cumulative effect of all the measures you put in place should create a comprehensive solution that embodies these critical qualities—based on our experience with financial institutions of all sizes.

Accuracy is first and foremost

The most important quality is clear—accuracy. All other qualities take a distant second place to accuracy. An employee fraud solution needs to be able to detect real evidence of fraud while minimizing false positives, which waste time and sap energy from your analysts and investigators. Accuracy means zeroing in on the fraud you know (e.g., scenarios shown to be indicative of fraud) as well as the fraud you don't even know is happening (e.g., unusual employee behavior that is outside the norm for a defined peer group, such as a specific job code).[57] Without accuracy, you can't be confident that your solution is finding fraud. And simply generating lots of alerts isn't the goal of an employee fraud solution, any more than simply generating a lot of notes is the goal of a musician.[58] The salient quality of a successful solution is that it needs to be able to generate the right kind of alerts—actionable alerts that lead to quick detection of (and protection from) fraud and recovery of stolen funds.

Accurate alerts matter

As one of our math teachers used to tell us back in elementary school, *close doesn't count except in horseshoes and hand grenades.* And Greg Leibon, our in-house mathematician,[59] agrees. "Much of the work in designing a fraud solution—for internal or external fraud threats—focuses on making it as accurate as possible," he says. "Without accuracy, you have nothing, really. Identifying outlier behaviors means you'll be able to identify outliers, not necessarily fraudsters. Detecting unusual activity just means a lot of alerts, not necessarily good ones. You need to be more than close—you need to achieve pinpoint accuracy."

Consider the importance of accuracy to your analysts and investigators. A flurry of large numbers of alerts can be self-defeating, distracting analysts and investigators from real evidence of fraud. False positives waste valuable time, money, energy, and focus. They can cause analysts and investigators to lose confidence in

---

[57] As we discussed earlier, unusual activity doesn't necessarily mean fraud, but it can be an early indicator of possible fraud.

[58] Or at least any musician you might want to listen to.

[59] Introduced in Chapter 8, Greg is an expert in applying advanced mathematical concepts to solving the challenges of fraud.

a solution, undermining your investment in it. Ultimately, the key fraud-fighting groups within your organization need to have faith that your fraud solution is accurate and capable of providing a steady flow of actionable alerts. Having confidence in the system allows them to take pride in their work, knowing they are performing a valuable service on behalf of the company and its clients.

Time after time, we've seen banks adding additional filters on to their fraud detection system to simply weed out the false positives. We think fraud detection systems should already be taking that critical step.

Remember that a lot of internal fraud mimics completely normal behavior and actions, so the system needs to be extremely smart (and able to get even smarter) to detect fraud among seemingly normal transactions. Your employee fraud solution needs to recognize the context of employee actions and detect the presence of fraud with the sensitivity and sophistication of a gourmet's palate or a hunting dog's nose (choose your metaphor). After all, if employee fraud were easy to detect, you'd already be detecting all of it. But employee fraud is a sophisticated, insidious, and damaging type of fraud, as we've shown. Accuracy ensures that your commitment to stopping employee fraud actually pays off with results—not just a perfunctory checkbox to placate regulators or shareholders.

Moving fast to stop fraudsters

Consider *time* carefully when thinking about employee fraud. Moving quickly to identify potential employee fraud is vital. After all, you want to stop fraudsters before the critical point where funds (or data) leave your bank. We call this the *point of value transfer*. This point can occur extremely quickly, such as when an employee initiates an illegal wire transfer of funds to an external member of a collusive gang. Or it can happen more slowly. For example, an employee might credit his own account with unauthorized fee reversals, accruing fraud earnings in his account. In this case, the funds are still within the realm of the bank, at least for a while.

Employee fraud is a game that moves and evolves as you play it. The rules change. The schemes become more complex.

The critical quality isn't the *fastest speed possible*. Speed has trade-offs. True real-time response is always a good thing, but may not be necessary. It can be overkill, and prohibitively expensive and complicated for certain types of fraud. After all, your investment should mirror your risk level. When addressing employee fraud, the key quality is that the system should be able to detect possible fraud *before the point of value transfer*. Ideally, you want to focus on *pre-loss* detection, which keeps the funds within your institution. That said, *post-loss* investigation and recovery can provide a second line of defense against employee fraud losses.

An efficient, fast solution enables your organization to keep pace with fraudsters, who are intent on transferring funds and data out of the walls of your institution as quickly as possible. Fraudulently obtained funds kept within your institution are evidence waiting to be discovered. So fraudsters move quickly to move their illicit gains elsewhere—to gang members who aren't employees, to resellers (e.g., online markets buying customer data), or to outside accounts. Your solution should move just as quickly to stop this transfer—whether it's thousands of dollars or thousands of customer Social Security numbers, addresses, or other data.

Flexibility helps you keep pace

Employee fraud is a game that moves and evolves as you play it. The rules change. The schemes become more complex. As fraudsters uncover new weaknesses, the word spreads virally and you'll find other fraudsters exploiting them across the industry. Get investigators and analysts together and they quickly start talking about what they're seeing at their institution, sharing how they're being targeted.

So employee fraud evolves quickly—like bad weather. A system that simply monitors for basic employee fraud scenarios, but doesn't have the flexibility to evolve, will quickly become outmoded, and circumvented by fraudsters. Remember, employees have inside knowledge of how your organization does everything—from transactional systems to internal controls. If your fraud detection solution remains static, fraudsters will quickly figure out what it's monitoring and (more importantly) what it's not monitoring.

For example, early insider fraud detection efforts centered on monitoring employee accounts alone. Of course, a great deal of employee fraud happens outside of their own accounts—so employee fraudsters quickly learn to use the accounts of relatives and friends to perpetrate their schemes. So the scope has expanded to customer accounts, General Ledger accounts, and far beyond.

In short, your employee fraud solution should always be capable of expanding and evolving to keep pace with, and stay ahead of, new developments in employee fraud. Your employee fraud solution can't simply monitor for the types of fraud you are finding today. That level of protection does nothing to proactively anticipate tomorrow's conditions, new fraud scenarios, complex collusive employee-external gangs, and other emerging threats.

Achieving this flexibility needs to be seamless, without requiring time-consuming IT involvement, a major programming investment, or other inherently slow-moving processes. Control of any system needs to rest largely with your fraud-fighting team members, since they are the ones experiencing new types of fraud and know best how to adjust the system to detect fraud going forward. However, this approach often is not the norm.

Ultimately, the solution you implement for employee fraud needs to deliver measurable value commensurate with its costs, achieving a ROI within what you determine to be an acceptable time period.

Delivering value

Accuracy, speed, and flexibility define the core qualities of an employee fraud-fighting solution. But there are other considerations that merit your attention.

Let's put the bottom line at the top of the list. After all, we're in a time when all costs are being carefully scrutinized, including investment in a system that detects and prevents employee fraud. The real issue isn't necessarily the pricetag of the investment, though it's important that the level of investment mirror your level of potential risk. Consider the total value[60] of addressing internal fraud—from reducing the revenues draining out of your institution to protecting it from reputational damage to reducing overall risk.

Ultimately, the solution you implement for employee fraud needs to deliver measurable value commensurate with its costs, achieving a ROI within what you determine to be an acceptable time period. You're looking for sustained success against an ongoing problem. So evaluating a solution means more than simply comparing the initial costs, but looking carefully at how the solution delivers value, year after year. After all, employee fraud is an ongoing challenge. Your solution should deliver ongoing results—and significant value.

---

[60] You'll find a more detailed discussion of value in Chapter 5.

Deft data management

We've discussed the importance of data in Chapter 9 and elsewhere. Data is both the lifeblood of fraud detection and a major challenge for the systems that detect it. The ability to access, manage, integrate, and search data effectively—and cost-effectively—is vital. A traditional data warehousing approach to data can be expensive, time-consuming, and complex to implement—and can be difficult to cost-justify.[61] So it's critical to examine how your employee fraud detection system deals with data. Is there a better way? Can you design a system that turns data from a burden into a blessing? Yes. And while data management might seem like a particularly technical topic best left to IT, it's not. Data is critical to your success in fighting fraud. And data management is critical to the efficiency and cost of that fight. So it merits attention at all levels—technical, organizational, and executive.

Where does control reside?

We discussed control briefly in the context of flexibility. Users should have the ability to adjust the solution to better match current and anticipated fraud threats. But this point raises a bigger question and issue worth exploring. What group within your organization is responsible for your employee fraud detection solution? Is this control centralized or shared among a committee? Do the actual users of the system—analysts and investigators—have control of this critical system, or at least a major voice in its ongoing evolution? Knowing the answers to these questions can tell you a lot about the eventual success of any current or prospective solution.

---

[61] Once you build the data warehouse, Murphy's Law dictates that key fields needed to fight fraud will have been omitted, and another costly project will be required to add those fields.

An integrated solution that encompasses all fraud threats

Though we are focusing on employee fraud here in *Insidious*, employee fraud doesn't exist in a vacuum—it's part of the overall continuum of fraud, one that includes external threats (e.g., credit card fraud and check fraud) as well as internal threats (i.e., employee fraud). The line between internal and external fraud frequently blurs, as employees enable outside collusive fraud gangs, outsiders seek to gain employment with the intent to commit fraud, and fraud schemes integrate multiple payment and/or delivery channels.

Having all fraud detection efforts managed on one integrated platform makes sense, because it recognizes the simple fact that all fraud is a threat. Fighting an enterprise problem effectively requires a collaborative approach that brings together all fraud threats, since they are often interrelated, as when smaller internal frauds enable larger external frauds.

Working with what you already have

Your solution should also integrate with all existing internal controls, without requiring a from-the-ground-up rethink of processes that are already in place— and working well.

Financial institutions are notorious for multiple and siloed systems. Fraud detection shouldn't follow suit. Fraud is an enterprise problem that stretches throughout and beyond all organizational divisions, channels, and products. Your fraud-detection strategy must encapsulate the needs of your enterprise to maximize effectiveness, and to protect your institution from the broadest array of threats.

Comprehensive capabilities

And finally, consider the scope of your employee fraud solution. Does it cover the two broad capabilities—fraud detection/prevention and investigation?[62] Does it bring you all the capabilities you need, from fraud detection and analysis to case management, forensic investigation, and reporting? Or will it require ancillary processes and supplemental solutions to give your analysts and investigators everything that they need to protect your institution from employee fraud threats?

An employee fraud solution that provides comprehensive capabilities is inherently easier to implement and manage than one patched together from disparate solutions. As your fraud-prevention needs expand, the system should be able to meet those needs too.

Qualities, not quantities

Accuracy. Speed. Flexibility. Value. Control. Integration. Comprehensive capabilities. These qualities and others add up to more than a wish list for an employee fraud solution. They can help you evaluate your current solution and any prospective solution you consider—and choose the best approach for your institution. After all, the goal of an employee fraud solution isn't to generate more alerts—it's to detect more fraud and minimize losses.

---

[62] Chapter 9 highlights the specifics of each capability.

CHAPTER ELEVEN

FIRST STEPS

"There are two mistakes one can make along the road to truth—not going all the way, and not starting."

—Buddha

Good morning. Welcome to work. Here's your coffee—don't worry, it's decaf. And here's your paper. Might want to check out the front page of the business section.

[Your Company Name Here] reports $41.5 million fraud loss
—Fraud ring uses insiders to steal from customers over two years, thousands of accounts affected—
Wow! You sure sprayed that coffee all over the office. Let me get some paper towels. Hey, your phone's ringing. Oh, it's the head of Investor Relations. He wants to talk to you. Sounds kind of angry. And look at all those emails on your Blackberry. It's going to be a really busy day.

Sound like a nightmare? It is. A major fraud loss is definitely one of the worries that keeps financial services executives up late at night. And when it's a public event, splashed on the front page of the newspaper, highlighted on television, or spread across the Internet, the damage multiplies. After all, a major fraud event isn't just about the revenues your institution loses. It can trigger customer defections, tarnish your reputation, and create a very expensive problem.[63]

We hear from a lot of banks in the wake of a high-dollar loss of funds or data. And it's safe to say that all of them wish they hadn't found themselves in such an uncomfortable, difficult situation. Reacting to an emergency doesn't put any business in a position of strength. That's why we advocate a proactive approach, both in business and in monitoring for fraud. It's always best to do what you can to stop fraud (and the subsequent losses, bad publicity, and other damage) *before* it happens.

---

[63] See Richard S. Levick's comments on damage control in Chapter 4.

Put in a medical context, do you wait until you're bleeding, nearly comatose, or in acute pain before you go to the doctor? Hope not.

Resist the urge to do nothing

That said, *stasis* is often the prevailing condition in human nature and business. Things tend to stay the same at banks, which are historically cautious and conservative. "I see a lot of denial out there, still," says one industry veteran. "Banks just don't want to admit that their own people might steal from them, even though it's increasingly obvious that every financial institution—and beyond—has some level of employee fraud, particularly now."

This tendency toward the status quo is changing, thanks to the tumultuous change in the financial markets, which require a more nimble response to ensure organizational survival. But like fraudsters, bank executives often need the powerful combination of opportunity and motivation[64] to take the first steps— in this case, to fight fraud, not commit it.

Take the opportunity to fight fraud

The opportunity is clear—fraud is not an intractable problem. There is a solution. And there are more systems, tools, strategies, partners, and advisors than ever available to help you protect your institution against employee fraud and other fraud threats. There's a growing awareness of fraud in general, thanks to high-profile cases. And that awareness has spawned a remarkable outpouring of knowledge and expertise, solutions, consultancies, industry publications, blogs, affinity groups, conferences, and much more. Technological breakthroughs— some fueled by Internet technologies, others by lower-cost computing, still others by old-fashioned innovation—put more power at your disposal to fight fraud. These breakthroughs enable lower-cost, higher-value solutions that can be implemented faster and deliver real value in days—not at the glacial pace of the past.

---

[64] The same elements required to commit fraud (as highlighted in Chapters 1 and 2) are also necessary to fight it. Coincidence? We don't think so.

You have an unparalleled opportunity to fight fraud. And you're not alone. As other institutions wrestle with the challenges of fraud, their knowledge is transforming into best practices. And when you survey the landscape of solutions, you'll find it has expanded significantly during the last few years.

But does that mean you'll take action? Maybe not. For that, you need the catalyzing ingredient, motivation.

Finding the motivation to fight employee fraud

Repeat after us—"My financial institution has an employee fraud problem." Find it hard to say? That's because no one wants to admit they have a problem, even if they didn't create it. But high-profile, high dollar loss fraud events aren't the only motivators for addressing employee fraud. And denial can always turn to acceptance, stasis into action. We're seeing more and more executives are facing up to the issue, and they're motivated by several key forces.

The first is financial. Employee fraud drains revenues, saps morale and productivity, and triggers customer flight. In highly competitive times, when financial institutions are focusing on the traditional work of attracting deposits, employee fraud is even more of a threat. This return to core business practices means fighting core threats—and employee fraud is about as close to the core as it gets. Plus, one of the core requirements of any institution is to create a superior work environment—one of mutual respect and minimal threats.

A move toward greater integrity

Without getting preachy, another powerful motivating factor is more about *doing the right thing*[65] than taking the path of least resistance and lowest investment— financial, organizational, and personal (e.g., doing nothing). You'll find plenty of executives deciding to fight fraud simply because it's the right thing to do, for their organization, its customers, and shareholders. In fact, roughly half of the recent graduating class from Harvard Business School signed an oath to "serve

---

[65] The Spike Lee film of the same name isn't the only instance of seeing choices in harsh but clarifying moral light.

the greater good, act with the utmost integrity and guard against decisions and behavior that advance my own narrow ambitions, but harm the enterprise and the societies it serves." [66] Considered by many to be the business equivalent of the Hippocratic Oath signed by physicians, it's clear that this high-profile development is part of a larger trend toward infusing business decisions with new integrity. Letting a fraud problem—one that harms employees, customers, investors, and the overall financial services industry—slide or go under-addressed would definitely not be allowed in this context.

No matter what their motivation, a growing number of banking executives are refusing to simply accept employee fraud as a cost of doing business. And they're deciding to do something about it.

The answer to fraud starts with one question
So first, the big question: [67]

Are you ready to address the challenge of employee fraud?

If you answer *no*, simply shut this book and go on with your day. Forget about fraud—until you have a big loss of revenues or data, find yourself in a public relations firestorm, or find that your worries about fraud are starting to make you lose a lot of sleep. Then you can simply open the book and keep reading.

If you answer *yes*, well—*congratulations*. You're taking that first step that begins every journey,[68] one that ultimately leads you to lower actual losses, protection against potential losses, and mitigated risk of reputational damage—plus a long list of other qualitative benefits, from greater efficiency to higher morale. But know that protecting your company against employee fraud is a long-term effort—not a one-time event. The threat of employee fraud is ongoing and evolving, so your efforts to fight it should be too.

---

[66] "A Hippocratic oath for managers," *The Economist*, June 4, 2009.
[67] Fans of *The Matrix* will recognize this as the "red pill/blue pill" moment.
[68] "A thousand-mile journey begins with a single step," Chairman Mao.

Where to start?

Your organization has already taken some steps toward protecting itself from internal fraud—including employee training, internal controls, monitoring systems, and other systems or processes. Surveying and assessing your existing infrastructure and ways of working sets a baseline for any changes you make and lets you leverage what you have in place. It's also a chance to identify which groups within your organization are responsible for monitoring for employee fraud, and protecting your organization (and its customers) from losses. Many times, this responsibility is shared between managers or groups. But it's important to know where responsibility resides.

Assessing your current protection level

Deciding to address employee fraud raises a wide range of questions right from the start:

Assessment of Risk: What are your current fraud losses, as well as your potential losses? Where are your most vulnerable areas? What areas need more vigilant monitoring? What level of investment is your organization making in fighting employee fraud today? What level of investment is justified when moving ahead (e.g., making the business case for investing in employee fraud).[69]

Assessment of Policies: Are your incentive policies actually encouraging fraud? Is your management compensation competitive enough to help reduce the temptation of high-level fraudsters? Are you taking current policy violations seriously? Are you allowing employees to stay after committing violations or even initial frauds? Is it clear to all employees, new-hires to veterans, that fraud isn't tolerated? Do you publicize (without raising the specter of Big Brother) the fact that employees are monitored for fraud? Do surprise audits actually happen? Do you have a confidential fraud hotline for tips, or in case an employee is coerced or threatened by organized criminal gangs? Coercion is a growing, disturbing trend. Do you insist that employees use their allotted vacation time? After all, fraudsters are legendary for refusing to go on vacation, lest their misdeeds come to light.[70]

---

[69] The Santa Fe Group offers a full report on this topic, available at: www.mementosecurity.com/news-events/library.php

[70] See the Afterword for an example of this tendency.

Truly deciding to address employee fraud means more than simply bolting on another auxiliary system to your current fraud-fighting machinery.

Assessment of Current Tools: Do your analysts and investigators have the tools and support they need? Are you monitoring all major data streams for evidence of fraud? Can your solution monitor all organizational levels or just tellers and customer service representatives? Are you monitoring employees by position to identify anomalous behaviors? And what metrics will you measure and chart to know that you're being successful in fighting employee fraud?[71]

We're not going to attempt to answer these questions. They're extremely specific to your organization and its unique situation. But you should see the initial stages of rethinking your employee fraud strategies as an opportunity for questioning, exploration, and realignment. Truly deciding to address employee fraud means more than simply bolting on another auxiliary system to your current fraud-fighting machinery. To truly change the amount of fraud you are uncovering and averting, you have to change the way you're fighting fraud.

Looking beyond your current efforts
In addition to looking inward, examining your current ways of working, and asking the right questions, your initial steps forward can also take you outside your organization. You might want to consider connecting with other financial institutions that are fighting fraud via industry forums, blogs, events, and other channels. After all, every financial institution faces employee fraud challenges, and many are extremely forthcoming about their experiences. Learn from them. Explore the solutions available now. Identify the best solution providers.

---

[71] We'll be talking more about value, results, and metrics in the next chapter.

Read the latest Gartner reports and other available literature. Talk to your analysts and investigators to get their perspective, since they're on the frontlines of fraud. And make sure that your fraud team is clearly identified and empowered to move ahead.

Changing your culture

Your efforts to fight employee fraud can change your culture from allowing employee fraud to go undetected to addressing it. You can change your overall culture by investing in fighting employee fraud, sending a strong anti-fraud message to new hires and veteran employees, providing effective training, and enforcing internal controls.

Changing a corporate culture can resemble turning an ocean liner. It's an effort that requires a unified front—from Human Resources to the Executive Team. The right signals throughout the company can help send a strong message that employee fraud isn't tolerated. This change may trigger some short-term challenges. For example, we recently identified an entire branch of a bank that was committing pretty damaging policy violations. Clearly, there were problems (and fraud) at this branch. But investigating and firing an entire branch may be counter-productive or impossible. What would your bank do?

You might have to be willing to take some short term hits—more terminations, some staff turmoil—to achieve the long term goal of a culture focused on solving employee fraud rather than ignoring it. In the end, the benefits of fighting employee fraud far surpass the significant costs and risks of tolerating it.

Looking back from a perspective of several years, you'll be very glad you took the first steps to address employee fraud. After all, employee fraud is just one element of the overall fraud continuum—one that's linked to a wide range of external fraud risks as well. The ability to address employee fraud is often an important foundation for other fraud-fighting efforts.

CHAPTER TWELVE

THE RESULTS

"However beautiful the strategy, you should occasionally look at the results."

—Winston Churchill

What do you want to get out of your efforts to fight employee fraud?

Ideally, this effort would eliminate fraud from your workplace. Employee fraud simply wouldn't be part of your organization. But employee fraud *does* happen.[72] And it's happening more and more, in increasingly diverse schemes, via new channels, and in collusion with outside fraudsters. Many of these internal elements of external fraud schemes remain hidden and undiagnosed, leading financial institutions to think that internal fraud isn't an issue. But it is. Your fraud detection efforts need to keep employee fraud at its lowest possible level, limiting losses and reducing risk from all types of fraud.

The results you can achieve fall into two main categories. There are qualitative organizational benefits—from greater organizational efficiency to higher morale. These benefits are important and powerful, but inherently hard to measure. And if you're going to invest in fighting employee fraud, you need to have some quantifiable, bottom-line metrics that help you know that you're making progress in this fight.

First, look at the dollars and data lost

The American Bankers Association[73] has convened a group to define the metrics for employee fraud, which will help answer the question of how to measure results. Luckily, there are already plenty of measurable areas. Let's start by taking a look at some of the main areas where results and value can be measured clearly. The most obvious is the overall fraud loss figure, measured in actual dollar losses linked to employee fraud (not incorrectly categorized as bad debt or included in another loss category). Monitoring this figure will let you measure actual reductions in fraud losses due to employee actions, which should, ultimately, go down.

---

[72] *Fraud Happens*—possible bumper sticker.

[73] www.aba.org.

The value paradox

Let's explore this phenomenon for a moment. If your people know that fraud isn't tolerated, that there are efficient monitoring systems in place, and that policies are enforced, then you should see a reduction in the actual number of incidents, actual losses, and policy violations. In short, the metrics get lower, not higher. This effect is often called the *value paradox*. Simply put, it means that as you address and invest in employee fraud, the actual *value* of the losses reduces. Does that mean the investment isn't working? No. It means that you've created a strong deterrent effect, one that's warding off significant potential losses. Banks with early-detection systems in place report minimal internal losses. And they're also reporting more funds recovered.

Calculating potential losses

Potential losses are also important, since fraud losses tend to accrue over time. Stopping fraud lowers the potential losses—losses that would have happened if your analysts and investigators hadn't identified fraud and stopped it. For example, a teller taking $10,000 a month might be detected in March after stealing $30,000. But the potential losses for the rest of the year (and beyond) might total $90,000 or more. It's important to project the value of loss avoidance created by detecting and terminating the employee when a clear pattern of theft exists.

In some cases, these potential losses are very clear, particularly with regular, ongoing fraud events of ever-escalating amounts. In other cases, it's less clear. For example, consider an employee who surfs five hundred accounts, gathering customer data that later led to account takeovers or new account fraud by outside fraudsters. It's harder to project the loss avoidance created by detecting and terminating that employee. Clearly, the financial services industry needs to come to agreement about an accurate method of measuring projected loss avoidance of all types.

Looking at recovered funds

On the *post-loss* side, the amount of funds recovered via the efforts of your investigators is also an important measure of success. Ideally, investigators should be able to get more funds back via effective investigations. Ideally, these funds would have never left your institution in the first place. But given the nature of fraud, you want to recover as much as possible of any fraud losses. For investigators, recovery is a critical measurement of success.[74]

It's important to recognize that dollars aren't the only valuable commodity at risk within your organization. Customer data is also vulnerable, and a popular target of fraud—one that can lead to actual dollar losses when outside fraudsters buy this data and use it to compromise accounts. If your employee fraud-fighting solution is working, the amount of customer data compromised or stolen by employees should also reduce.

Measuring the number of fraudsters

On the *people* side of evaluating your fraud-fighting efforts, you can measure the number of employees who have been identified, investigated, and judged to be fraudsters—either by internal review or investigation by law enforcement. This number records the actual population of known employee fraudsters—across all departments and branches.

Clear measures include the number of confessions, terminations, and convictions related to fraud—as well as the number of Suspicious Activity Reports (SARs) filed. If you're fighting employee fraud effectively, these figures should trend downward over time. However, you might find an initial spike in this number when you implement more effective fraud-fighting solutions and systems and uncover longstanding fraud schemes that previously went undetected.

---

[74] Investigators gauge their success, and their value to the bank, by the funds they are able to recover, as discussed in Chapter 9.

Measuring alerts and their accuracy

As we highlighted in Chapter 10, accuracy is the most important quality of a solution designed to protect your organization from employee fraud. But how can you measure accuracy? Accuracy isn't measured by the sheer volume of alerts, since false positives are a time-wasting, money-losing distraction. Instead, look at the ratio of alerts to investigations. Ideally, it should be 1:1, but that's in a perfect world. There will always be some alerts that need to be evaluated, and that can uncover important trends and valuable information, but that don't lead to investigations. But the number of false positives (alerts that don't lead to investigations) should reduce over time, indicating greater efficiency and accuracy.

Keeping false positives low raises the productivity of your analysts and investigators, ensures that they have faith in the alerts that they receive, and helps them do their work more efficiently.

Fewer, more efficient investigations

When you begin addressing employee fraud in a serious, committed way, your investigators may find themselves handling more investigations that lead to more terminations. They will be working more cases. In the end, though, the real goal is more prevention and fewer investigations. With the right system in place—and an anti-fraud culture instilled in your people—there should be fewer investigations. So tracking the number of investigations (i.e., actual cases) that are being handled is a clear measure of success in the fight against employee fraud.

These investigations should be as efficient as possible. The duration of investigations should reduce, as fraud is identified earlier. It's easier, less time-consuming, and less costly, to investigate a fraud scheme that's been underway for three weeks vs. three years. Individual investigators will be able to handle more cases per investigator in this environment, since cases become simpler and can be worked more quickly. They will also be able to focus on a broader range of fraud issues, both external and internal.

Measuring real value

The measures described here are all helpful in your effort to assess the effectiveness of your fight against employee fraud. Taken together, and over time, these numbers give you a clear idea of the value of fighting employee fraud. But what might real-world results look like? Let's take a look at some actual results that financial institutions have achieved by addressing employee fraud.

Early detection, lower losses

One smaller bank[75] serves as a microcosm of the overall impact of monitoring for fraud more vigilantly. In the past, its normal number of internal fraud incidents averaged 52 a year, with an average loss of $54,500 per incident. After making a commitment to address internal fraud—and implementing proactive monitoring —the bank reports that it is finding an average of 75 employees committing fraud each year. So it can detect increasing amounts of fraud. But more importantly, the average loss per incident is $29,700. While the overall dollar amounts in this case are relatively small, the percentile reduction is impressive. By detecting fraud earlier, more vigilant monitoring cuts fraud losses in half. Multiplied out over multiple fraudsters at a large bank, the loss reductions can total millions of dollars.

The bottom line? Catching more fraud earlier helps reduce losses significantly.

Tapping the power of proactive monitoring

Now let's turn to a larger bank, one with more than $700 billion in assets, and 610 million transactions a day. After a major internal fraud event in 2005, this industry leader took a hard look at how it was addressing internal fraud. It saw internal fraud as a major problem. And it considered addressing employee fraud as part of its commitment to protecting its customers' accounts and information.

---

[75] For confidentiality reasons, we can't name institutions directly.

The bottom line? Catching more fraud earlier helps reduce losses significantly.

The commitment to addressing employee fraud came from the highest levels of the company, and ultimately resulted in roll-out of a new, more powerful solution for monitoring—one capable of handling the bank's significant data volume. One key measure of success and the value of this implementation falls under the general category of empowering investigators. In the past, investigators might have to wait hours or days for a mainframe search when pursuing employee fraud. Now information is available at their fingertips in seconds, enabling more efficient, productive investigations.

Capabilities like these enable the bank to identify and stop employee fraud faster. For example, a 2006 identity theft scheme involving a teller cost the bank more than $1 million in losses. Early identification and intervention kept a similar event in 2008 to $58,000 in losses. "The central benefit of more accurate, proactive monitoring for us is that it lets us identify fraudulent activity more quickly, reducing our losses significantly," says one corporate fraud veteran at the bank.

Spotting inappropriate activities and fraud before they escalate helps reduce the bank's employee fraud losses by several million dollars a year. Plus, it protects the bank's reputation.

Consider these real-world results from banks and credit unions that have committed to addressing employee fraud—and implemented vigilant proactive monitoring:

Debiting General Ledger Accounts

Three associates in the same branch were terminated after performing debits to a miscellaneous fee GL account.

The Results:
Three employees terminated
Identified loss: $100,250
Loss averted: $501,675

Making Account Inquiries and Selling Account Holder Information

A teller in Georgia was identified selling information on high-balance account holders to a NJ fraud ring.

The Results:
Organized crime ring uncovered
Loss stopped at $55,000
Loss averted: More than $1,000,000

Stealing from Private Banking Clients

A 20-year veteran bank employee was identified stealing from private banking clients in $500 to $1,500 increments.

The Results:
Identified loss: $107,000
Averted loss: > $1,175,000 (including direct loss averted and reputational damage)

Self Dealing by Performing Debits and Credits on Employee Accounts

At one very large financial institution, automated proactive monitoring identified more than 500 employees performing debits and credits on their own accounts.

The Results:
Incidents ranged from policy and code of conduct violations to theft

Employee Steals Credit Card Account Data

An analyst identified an employee accessing multiple credit card accounts, which subsequently reported fraudulent transactions. A bank investigator interviewed the employee and obtained a confession that this account data was supplied to an external fraud ring.

The Results:
Loss: $1,243,000
Employee terminated and turned over to law enforcement

Teller Misuses Position to Make Early TDA Withdrawals

A teller was identified making early withdrawals from Time Deposit Accounts (TDAs) in $9,900 increments—and waiving fees.

The Results:
Identified loss: $89,000 plus $500 in waived fees
Averted loss: Regulatory fines

Employee Steals Funds from Wealthy Clients

An analyst identified an employee with excessive refunds to their own checking account. An investigator determined that the employee was stealing from the General Ledger as well as taking funds from several wealthy clients.

The Results:
Identified loss: $66,100+
Employee terminated and turned over to law enforcement

These are just some of the types of results and value your institution can gain from addressing employee fraud. While the results will vary, we see significant quantifiable benefits when banks address employee fraud. And we see analysts who are uncovering new, emerging schemes every day and shutting them down—stopping and averting major losses.

Back to those more qualitative considerations

Our final point on value is more philosophical than measurable—employee fraud shouldn't be tolerated at any level, measurable or not. What's the value of ridding your organization of thieves who steal from your company and its customers? What's the value of having a productive workforce where people feel confident that their colleagues are there to work, not steal? What's the value of a management structure that takes internal controls, ethics, and honesty seriously?

Ultimately, taking employee fraud seriously brings value to your organization on two levels. It helps you attract great employees who respect and believe in your bank. And it sends a strong message to customers that your bank takes its special responsibility of protecting them and their money seriously—a message that can be a strong differentiator in the marketplace.

"MY BANK SHOULD HAVE CAUGHT ME A LONG TIME AGO."

The work of identifying employee fraud can be pretty abstract—bringing together data sets, establishing fraud scenarios, identifying unusual behaviors among groups of employees.

But as investigators will tell you, it's also a very human problem. To conclude *Insidious,* we took the unusual step of calling a fraudster and letting her tell us (and you) more about the problem in her own words.

Donna Lee Munson[76] is a former assistant vice president at a bank in Georgia, who was caught and convicted of stealing almost $200,000 from her bank. She worked for her bank for ten years, and was an integral part of the bank and her community. She's married with three children. Her voice was shaky and soft, with occasional tears and silences, as she described the path that led her from a successful career in banking to a nightmarish life fraught with fear of detection. In the period before and after her trial, Donna withdrew from the world and thought long and hard about the actions that led her to this point—actions she clearly wishes she had never taken.

We spoke with her just weeks before she began serving an 18-month sentence at a federal facility in North Carolina.

Did you like working at your bank?
I loved it. It was very family-oriented. I was in the public. Got to see people all day. I met tons of people on a daily basis that became very close friends of ours. I loved my staff. We'd do things together on the weekends. My kids would babysit their younger kids. We were one big family. It wasn't just a bunch of employees.

---

[76] At her request, we have changed her name and small details of her story.

Did you feel like you were well-treated by the bank and its management?
Perfect. You couldn't ask for anything better.

Getting to the specifics of what happened, you were transferring money from CDs into your own account, is that right?
Correct. I never took any cash. Cash seemed wrong to me. Cash seemed like a tool of my job. But the paper part of it just seemed different.

Eventually a CD comes due and there's a point where it's clear that the money's missing. Were you thinking that you'd repay it?
Absolutely, I always intended to repay it. It started in little amounts and it seemed like I could repay it and it's not going to be a big deal. But then it was more, and then it was more, and then it just got out of hand. It got to the point where I couldn't repay it in a timely way that no one would have ever noticed.

Was there a certain day when the pressure became too much and you decided to start committing fraud?
No. I don't remember that particular day. I don't remember waking up in the morning and going: *Okay. Today's the day that I'm going to do it.* It just sort of happened. I remember doing it that day and I was *sick* all day. And all night. I wanted to take it back the next morning. Wish that I hadn't done it. I didn't do it again for a good few months, because I was overwhelmed with guilt. It was *horrible*. And then it got to the point where it was like—steal or don't have a place for my kids to live. We have a daughter who started college. A son in high school. And a younger daughter.

The first time, how much was it?
It was like $300 the first time.

And what did it work its way up to?
Never more than $1,000. Well, I take that back, maybe $1,500. But they were small amounts.

You mentioned that it got out of hand. Was it just that it was so easy, or it didn't seem real? What contributed to the escalation of the whole process?

Both of those. Not getting caught was one. It just seemed that, well, nobody's picking up on it so it just seemed easier to do.

That must have been incredibly stressful.

It was very stressful. I worked every day of the week because I was afraid to take a day off. I was afraid somehow it would get caught. When we took vacations I always figured I would come back and not have my job. I always checked to see if there were different cars in the parking lot. Every single morning, to see if there was anybody out of the ordinary there waiting for me.

Did that have a physical effect on you?

Yes. It was very...you know, we laugh about being psychotic over it [breaks down, cries]. At the same time, my father passed away. That kind of did me in.

And on top of this, you were in serious financial crisis too.

Yes. We were put into a mortgage that we couldn't afford. That was our fault, and I blame ourselves. But I also blame the system a little bit.

So basically you had this mortgage that you were under water on. You had a good job, but it probably wasn't paying quite enough to cover everything.

No. And that's just it. I think people assumed that being an assistant vice president branch manager of a bank that you're making good money. When I left there, after ten years of being in this bank, I was only making about $40,000 a year. So I was not, by any means, getting rich off of the salary from this bank. People just assumed I was making a ton of money.

Did you find it hard with your co-workers? You were looking them in the eye and knowing that you were doing this. Was that hard?

Very.

Did they ever ask questions?
Never. They never asked a single question.

Now that this is public, have you talked with your co-workers? How do you address it with them?
I have not talked with any of them. They were actually told that they were to have no contact with me. I know the bank can't tell them that, but it was kind of: no contact or else.

That must be hard. They were your close friends.
At this point, I basically feel like I have no friends. Even my very best friend in the whole world works for that bank.

And you haven't talked to your best friend?
Nope. My husband has talked to her husband. But we've had no contact with her for fear...I would just die if anything was to happen to her job.

Did the bank have internal controls or monitoring? Something that was in place that you knew about that would keep this from happening?
Yes.

Why didn't they work?
I don't know.

Eventually, how did you get caught?
I took a day off. One of the customers that I personally dealt with on a daily basis, or weekly basis—he always came in to see me. I wasn't there and he ended up going to see somebody else and had a question about one of his CDs that I had taken money from, and that's how I got caught.

What would you tell someone considering committing employee fraud?

Don't do it. It's not worth it. Go to your family first.

How about banks? What would you tell them? Should they have better systems that catch this sort of thing?

Yes. I think so. They should have caught me a long time ago.

Do you think there are more people in your sort of situation?

I think so. There are lots of people out there who are just like me, who aren't felons or bad people. They just found themselves in a situation where they felt that that's what they needed to do. I bet they wish they hadn't either.

If you had to characterize this, this had been a monumentally life changing experience for you, yes?

Without a doubt.

And if you knew then what you know now, you wouldn't have done it?

No. No way.

Anything else that you want to pass along?

I live in a constant nightmare. I'm almost to the point where I'm agoraphobic. I don't leave my house. I'm afraid to run into people. I know so many people from my job. We live in a small community. We don't live in New York City where there's hundreds and thousands of people. We live in a small community where everybody knows everybody and goes to school with everybody and works with everybody. Thank goodness I have a son who drives and will go to the grocery store and do those things for me because I don't even leave the house.

You mentioned that one customer. You would never walk up to that guy on the street and take his money, would you?

Never. And I would never have taken a one dollar bill from the bank ever in my life. It just doesn't make any sense to me now to look back and think about what I did.

We ended our call drained and saddened by Donna Lee Munson's ordeal, the impact that fraud has had on her life, which has been forever changed by a bad, but understandable decision.

We weren't surprised by Donna's story, which confirmed many of the basic tenets of employee fraud—that it starts small, grows larger over time, and involves a lot of deception. We weren't surprised to find that Donna had perfectly sound motivations for committing fraud—a bad mortgage, rising debt, plus a personal crisis. And we weren't surprised that whatever basic monitoring her bank had in place didn't detect even this most basic and obvious fraud. After all, if monitoring and controls worked all the time, employee fraud wouldn't be on the rise.

Fraud is damaging in many ways

What surprised us was this—after spending years fighting employee fraud, developing technologies and implementing systems designed to catch the thousands of Donna Lee Munsons of the world, *we felt truly sorry for her.* We recognized that her fraud marked a significant failure of personal responsibility. And we know that financial institutions can only do so much to protect desperate employees from themselves. But it would take a cold-hearted person to not empathize with her story and its painful repercussions.

Employee fraud is a human problem that damages not only banks and customers, but also the employees caught stealing, their colleagues, their families, and their communities. It's a major challenge that merits attention and investment to ward off the damage—which can definitely be avoided with better protection, proactive monitoring, functional internal controls, and an anti-fraud culture.

We learned a great deal from our discussion with Donna Lee Munson, whom we consider an Everywoman of Fraud—not a career criminal, not a demon, just someone who actually found herself slipping over to the other side, committing fraud over two years. During that time, she took almost $200,000 from her bank and its customers, damaged its reputation, violated a crucial trust with her employer of ten years, shocked her customers, coworkers, and family, and derailed her life. In the end, she says it wasn't worth it. And we agree.

We hope that her words—among the last in our book—move you as much as they did us—and help convince you of the value of addressing the very real, very human, and inherently insidious problem of employee fraud.